Communications
in Computer and Information Science   447

T0212834

Markus Helfert   Brian Donnellan
Jim Kenneally (Eds.)

Design Science: Perspectives from Europe

European Design Science Symposium, EDSS 2013
Dublin, Ireland, November 21-22, 2013
Revised Selected Papers

 Springer

Volume Editors

Markus Helfert
Dublin City University, Ireland
E-mail: markus.helfert@computing.dcu.ie

Brian Donnellan
Maynooth University, Co. Kildare, Ireland
E-mail: brian.donnellan@nuim.ie

Jim Kenneally
Intel Labs Europe, Leixlip, Co. Kildare, Ireland
E-mail: jim.kenneally@intel.com

ISSN 1865-0929   e-ISSN 1865-0937
ISBN 978-3-319-13935-7   e-ISBN 978-3-319-13936-4
DOI 10.1007/978-3-319-13936-4
Springer Cham Heidelberg New York Dordrecht London

Library of Congress Control Number: 2014959118

Typesetting: Camera-ready by author, data conversion by Scientific Publishing Services, Chennai, India

Printed on acid-free paper

Springer is part of Springer Science+Business Media (www.springer.com)

Preface

This book contains papers presented at the European Design Science Symposium 2013, organized by the Innovation Value Institute (www.ivi.ie), the Business Informatics Group at Dublin City University (`http://big.computing.dcu.ie/`), and Intel Labs Europe (www.intel.eu/labs); held in conjunction with the Intel Ireland Research Conference (IIRC), the Irish Chapter of the Association for Information Systems (IAIS), (`http://www.iais.ul.ie/`), and the European Industry University Research Association (EIURA) (`http://www.eiura.org/`).

The purpose of the symposium is to bring together researchers and practitioners interested in practical aspects of design science research that has become an important approach for research and practice in the information systems discipline with a dramatic growth in recent related literature. Design science creates and evaluates IT artifacts intended to solve organizational problems that are identified. Such artifacts are represented in a structured form that may vary from software, formal logic, and rigorous mathematics to informal natural language descriptions. The rich phenomena that emerge from the interaction of people, organizations, and technology need to be qualitatively assessed to yield an understanding of the issues adequate for theory development or problem solving.

In addition to regular research papers, in EDSS 2013 we had two distinguished keynote presentations from leading thinkers in design science. In the first keynote presentation, Robert Winter provided a common foundation and integration of descriptive and design-oriented research in information systems. In his keynote he proposed a framework that is not only organized along the well-known "descriptive vs. prescriptive" dimension, but also introduces a generality dimension. The four resulting quadrants "operations," "explanations," "technologies," and "solutions" allow one not only to position all central objects of research, but also to position and better integrate research activities and iterations.

In the second keynote presentation, Alan Hevner presented an overview of foremost design science research and explored the readiness of innovation practice to include design science concepts and processes. He illustrated how at a recent conference, an initial round of a Delphi study engaged a number of innovation practitioners in a discussion around the question, "Is design science the future of innovation?" The results of the study were presented as summaries of opportunities and challenges in bringing design science into innovation practice, proposing a design science model of innovation, and utilizing Gregor's and Hevner's recent work on a common framework for categorizing innovation, i.e., knowledge innovation matrix.

In addition to these two keynote presentations, the Program Committee selected after the review process ten research papers for presentations at the symposium. All papers were reviewed by members of an international Program Committee.

We wish to extend our appreciation to our distinguished speakers and contributors. We hope you will find the papers in this book interesting and valuable and we hope they represent a helpful reference in the future for all those who need to address challenges related to design science mentioned above.

October 2014

Markus Helfert
Brian Donnellan
Jim Kenneally

Organization

The European Design Science Symposium (EDSS) 2013 was presented by Intel Labs Europe in association with the Innovation Value Institute and the Business Informatics Group at Dublin City University.

General Chairs

Martin Curley · Intel/Innovation Value Institute, Ireland
Alan Hevner · University of South Florida, USA

Program Chairs

Markus Helfert · Dublin City University, Ireland
Brian Donnellan · Maynooth University/Innovation Value Institute, Ireland

Industry Chair

Jim Kenneally · Intel

Local Organizing Chair

Aline Dijon · Intel

Program Committee

Par Agerfalk · Uppsala University, Sweden
Auinger Andreas · University of Applied Sciences, Upper Austria, Austria
Stephan Aier · University of St. Gallen, Switzerland
Liam Bannon · University of Limerick, Ireland
Sven Carlsson · Lund University, Sweden
Gabriel Costelloe · Galway-Mayo Institute of Technology, Ireland
Martin Curley · Intel/Innovation Value Institute, Ireland
Edward Curry · DERI - National University of Ireland, Galway, Ireland
Frank Devitt · Maynooth University, Ireland
Brian Donnellan · Maynooth University, Ireland

Table of Contents

Towards a Framework for Evidence-Based and Inductive Design in Information Systems Research*

Robert Winter

University of St. Gallen, Institute of Information Management
Müller-Friedberg-Strasse 8, CH-9000 St. Gallen
robert.winter@unisg.ch

Abstract. Discussions about design science research as an alternative or at least complementary approach to the dominant descriptive research paradigm have not only taken place in information systems research, but also in organizational sciences, accounting, operations, and other business research disciplines. In contrast to the descriptive research paradigm that can be taken over from sociology and psychology in a very mature state, the problem-solving paradigm is comparably new to business research. Not only have different variants of this approach (e.g. design as search, evidence-based design, emergent design) been proposed and applied that appear to be incompatible at first sight. Descriptive research and design science research also appear to have no common ground and no synergy potentials. As a consequence, not only seem improvement and change ('design and engineering') often detached from phenomenon analysis and theory building. The role of 'un-grounded', innovative practices is also not clear. In order to provide a common ground and support a better integration of descriptive and design-oriented research in information systems, we propose a framework that is not only organized along the well-known 'descriptive vs. prescriptive' dimension, but also introduces a generality dimension. The four resulting quadrants 'operations', 'explanations', 'technologies' and 'solutions' allow not only to position all central objects of research, but also to position and better integrate research activities and iterations. This extends not only to 'deductive' design (solution search based as well as evidence-based), but also to 'inductive' design.

1   Introduction

Information systems (IS) can be studied from two fundamentally different perspectives. The descriptive perspective aims at analyzing, explaining and / or at least partially predicting technology use by organizations and organizational actors as empirical phenomena. This research perspective dominates in social sciences and humanities. Its dominant outcomes are "theories for analysis, explanation and / or prediction" [2]. Examples from IS research are studies that explain why IS are used or

---

* The proposed framework is regarded to be applicable for information systems research as well as in related fields. In [1] the author describes the framework's application for organizational design and engineering. Most figures are identical.

M. Helfert et al. (Eds.): EDSS 2013, CCIS 447, pp. 1–20, 2014.

not continuously used [e.g. 3]. Such explanations may or may not include predictions of continuous use under changed conditions.

In contrast, the problem-solving, 'design' or 'engineering' perspective aims at improving IS use. Its dominant outcomes are "theories for design and action" [2]. Baskerville and Pries-Heje [4] present Walls et al.'s design theory for vigilant EIS [5] as an exemplar because it shows that certain templates, directives, etc. will ensure a consistent vision that allows executives to deal with their broad, diverse and variable issues. We will use the term design to characterize design as well as engineering aspects in the following. In contrast to the descriptive perspective, the design perspective is not restricted to analyzing existing empirical phenomena and is not purpose-free. Instead, it aims at creating 'better worlds', the ends for which effective means are proposed.

While the descriptive perspective dominates in important IS research communities (e.g. in the United States), the design perspective dominates in others [6]. Due to different positions, goals and outputs, it is not surprising that descriptive research and design research are considered to be disjunctive approaches [7, 8]. As an example, constructs in descriptive research are usually identified and validated in a completely different way than their counterparts in design research, leading to knowledge components that might be incompatible so that the findings built on such constructs cannot be combined or integrated. An exemplary 'mismatch' is the incompatibility between technology acceptance model constructs – like intention to use – that describe by what factors acceptance can be captured in a causal model on the one hand, and constructs that are used to describe methods for IS introduction on the other hand.

Missing integration between descriptive and design research impede cumulative research within and between communities, not only in IS research. This article therefore deals with the conceptual integration of descriptive and design research. A central challenge is to identify or propose a common conceptual basis that serves as a foundation for both research perspectives. Thus the first research goal of this article is to analyze related work on research frameworks regarding their integration suitability.

A second research question is related to the form in which generalized problem solutions are created in design research. Often a deductive approach is regarded as essential, i.e. proposed solutions should be based on generalized descriptive knowledge. In their "anatomy of a design theory", Gregor and Jones demand to always specify a "justificatory" or "kernel" theory, i.e. "the underlying knowledge or theory from the natural or social or design sciences that gives a basis and explanation for the design" [9]. Design, however, not always needs to be done in such an 'evidence-based' manner only. The inherently inductive approach of identifying and reusing patterns has not only been proposed in civil engineering [e.g. 10], but also in software engineering [e.g. 11] and organizational engineering [see e.g. 12, 13] – i.e. in reference disciplines of design-oriented IS research. The apparent benefit of inductive design is that yet 'unexplained' or 'un-grounded', innovative practices can be generalized and reused without have to take the 'detour' of descriptive theorizing. It is however unclear how inductive design should be structured from a conceptual research process perspective and which components of inductive design can be integrated with traditional design-oriented or with descriptive research activities. Thus the second research question of this article is how to integrate inductive design into the proposed conceptual framework.

Based on a common foundation of artifact types in social sciences and their use on the one hand, and generality levels of artifacts on the other, a two-dimensional model is introduced in the next section 'Common Foundation'. The proposed model's four quadrants 'operations', 'explanations', 'technologies' and 'solutions' allow not only to position all main objects of all mentioned research perspectives, but also to position and compare research processes and iterations in section 'Design and Engineering Activities'. In section 'De-Contextualization and Emergence', inductive design activities are characterized and integrated into the proposed framework. The concluding section discusses the proposal's contribution and suggests avenues for further research.

2   Common Foundation

In design science research for IS (DSR-IS), March and Smith's [14] differentiation of constructs, models, methods and instantiations as artifact types is commonly accepted [15]. Hevner et al. characterize these artifact types as follows: "Constructs provide the language in which problems and solutions are defined and communicated [...]. Models use constructs to represent a real world situation – the design problem and its solution space [...]. Methods define processes. They provide guidance on how to solve problems, that is, how to search the solution space. [...] Instantiations show that constructs, models, or methods can be implemented in a working system." [16]. Since models can not only represent problem solution requirements or problem solutions (means or ends, problem-solving paradigm), but also represent the phenomena under analysis (descriptive paradigm), we differentiate between 'problem or solution models' and 'descriptive models'.

As stated by Winter [6] it is important to understand the artifact types not as disparate concepts, but as an interlinked system. Chmielewicz's [17] taxonomy may serve as a foundation to explain such linkages. He differentiates between four fundamentally different research approaches in social sciences which build upon another: (1) ontology building, (2) theory building, (3) technology building and (4) judgment. The respective research outcomes in Chmielewicz's system are

- ontological facts (foundational concepts, e.g. constructs of a causal relationship, constructs of a problem requirements specification or constructs of a solution)
- theoretical statements (cause-effect relations, e.g. explanatory theories)
- technological statements (means-end relations, e.g. solution methods or solution models) and
- normative statements (object-value relations, e.g. evaluations of solution models).

Due to their conceptual differences, these types of outcomes can be regarded as fundamentally different artifact types. Descriptive models (theoretical statements) use constructs (ontological facts) as their building blocks. Problem or solution models as well as solution methods (technological statements) should use theory as explanatory justification. Actual solutions (model or method instantiations) are instantiated from technologies based on specific choices (judgment).

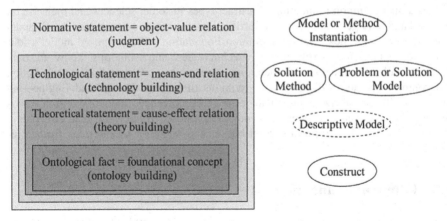

Artifact types (and research approaches)
following [Chmielewicz 1994]

Artifact types in design science
research for information systems

Fig. 1. Artifact types / research approaches in social sciences (left) and design science research for IS (right) [Based on 6, 18]

Fig. 1 relates the Chmielewicz taxonomy of artifact types and research approaches in social sciences (left) to the artifact types of the "Sciences of the Artificial" (DSR-IS, right). Foundational concepts can be related to constructs, theoretical statements can be related to descriptive models, means-end relations can be related to solution methods and problem / solution models, and object-value relations (= technologies chosen to achieve certain goals) can be related to model / method instantiations. The comparison supports three interesting insights [6]:

Firstly, the systems of research outcome types (and thus research activities) in social sciences and 'sciences of the artificial' seem to be more compatible than expected – given the fundamentally different perspectives of these approaches and the apparent lack of established common frameworks.

Secondly, descriptive models can and should be incorporated into the set of DSR-IS artifact types 'between' technological statements and ontological facts. This claim is supported by many authors [e. g., 5, 9, 19, 20] who argue that technology design should be informed by kernel / justificatory knowledge and, as a consequence, both should be based on the same conceptual foundation.

Thirdly, problem or solution models and solution methods are more closely related to each other than to other DSR-IS artifact types. It has in fact been argued that problem / solution models and solution methods are "two views of the same thing" [21]. While problem / solution models focus on design inputs and outputs – and imply procedural aspects –, solution methods focus on procedural aspects – and imply design outcomes. Some authors therefore propose to represent procedural aspects and outcomes in a more integrated forms, e. g. by process deliverable diagrams (for an exemplary application cf. [22]).

2.1 Descriptive vs. Prescriptive Artifacts

Descriptive models (including their constructs) are different from solution methods, problem / solution models and instantiations (including their constructs): Descriptive artifacts exist independently from any valuations or goals. As a consequence, (explanatory and / or predictive) theory building is aiming to propose primarily valid – and not necessarily useful – results. In contrast, solution methods as well as problem / solution models (including their constructs) are always related to certain (problem solution) goals, and instantiations are always created based on certain valuations and choices. As a consequence, technology development is aiming to propose primarily useful – and not necessarily valid - results.

Traditionally, only descriptive models that represent explanatory and / or predictive relations between constructs, have been designated as theory [cf. e. g. 23]. Since the term theory is claimed by all research paradigms, generic solution models and solution methods have also been designated theories in the context of DSR-IS [cf. e. g. 2, 9, 24, 25]. According to Gregor, the distinctive feature of a design theory is that it makes explicit prescriptions (e.g., construction guidelines, principles of form and function) for an artifact. Based on this specific feature, design theories can be understood as means-end relations according to the Chmielewicz taxonomy, as opposed to (explanatory) theories that are included as cause-effect relations in the taxonomy.

The question whether a design theory is just "effective practice" or has components whose validity can be proven, has been investigated by Baskerville and Pries-Heje [4]. They propose to separate a design theory into an explanatory and a practice component, designated as "explanatory design theory" and "design practice theory", respectively. From an explanatory point of view, design theory is "...a general design solution to a class of problems that relates a set of general components to a set of general requirements" [4] – this comes very close to Chmielewicz' understanding of generic means-end relations. Certain solution requirements can be interpreted as reasons for corresponding solution components. Certain solution components can be justified by corresponding solution requirements. While the explanatory design theory provides functional explanations for prescriptive artifacts, the design practice theory gives explicit prescriptions on how to design and develop an artifact, e.g. by applying solution methods and / or re-using (reference) solution components (e.g., patterns).

Theory is an important constituent for research, from a descriptive perspective as well as from a design perspective. It should be carefully differentiated whether "theory-type" statements relate cause and effect (explanatory and / or predictive theory) or relate means and ends (design theory). This line separates two 'worlds', the world of descriptive artifacts and the world of prescriptive artifacts.

2.2 Artifacts on Different Abstraction Levels

In the light of the huge amounts of highly diverse artifacts that are created both in design research and in design practice, the differentiation of descriptive and prescriptive artifacts seems not to be sufficient for a precise differentiation of research processes and outcomes. We therefore propose to additionally differentiate artifacts on different levels of abstraction. While instantiations represent one situated artifact implementation in context and time (e. g. a specific project plan or a specific workflow instance or a specific algorithm at a certain point in time), all other artifact types such as solution methods, solution models, descriptive models, or constructs can be instantiated by a set of more or less complex artifacts that are linked to more or less diverse goals, subject to more or less diverse contexts, valid in more or less points in time, etc.

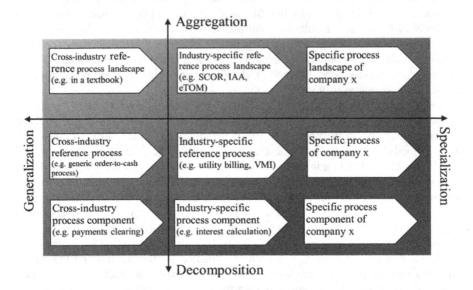

Fig. 2. Process models of different abstraction levels

In order to specify "more or less" abstraction, we refer to traditional data management approaches [e.g. 26] that differentiate at least a generalization / specialization and an aggregation / decomposition sub-dimension: While the level of generality indicates how many different instantiations the artifact allows, the level of aggregation indicates into how many components the artifact can be decomposed. MIT's process compass [27] is a nice example to illustrate that generalization / specialization and aggregation / decomposition are orthogonal sub-dimensions which specify the abstraction level of – in this case – a process model. Fig. 2 illustrates the process compass idea. A lighter background color indicates more general and / or more aggregate process models. A darker background color indicates more specific and / or more decomposed process models. Some exemplary process models are positioned in Figure 2 to illustrate not only their different degree of generalization / specialization and of aggregation / decomposition, but also to show that these dimensions are independent and all combinations exist.

The proposed two-dimensional abstraction model cannot only be applied to solution models (like process models). Exemplified by Business Process Management (BPM), typical abstraction levels for a solution method are

- Generic: Generality level is "one size fits all", i. e. the method is applicable to all processes in all organizations in all existing or possible worlds. Aggregation level is "one method covers all", i. e. the method is comprised of process analysis, process control, continuous process development and maybe even more components and thus covers modeling, performance management, change management, etc. BPM methods on this abstraction level are e.g. found in textbooks or method handbooks.

- Archetypal: The method is applicable for all problem situations that share certain properties (e.g. process type, organization type, project type/goals, available resources and/or skills). Usually a small number of problem archetypes is differentiated that represent important, relevant *design problem classes* like e. g. small enterprises, a certain industry, or certain BPM goals like speed or throughput. BPM methods on this generality level might be derived by adapting abstract methods to the problem class at hand and / or by selecting certain components of abstract methods.
- Configurable: Based on either a refinement of archetypes or on a classification of real-world problems, a large number of problem configurations is differentiated whose solutions are created from reusable modules by configuration or aggregation. BPM methods on this level of generality might either be inductively created from "best practices" or constructed as adaption of more general, e.g. archetype-specific methods. For BPM, a configurable method has been proposed by Bucher and Winter [28, 29]. They differentiate four archetypes of BPM, five resulting BPM project types, and show how three important BPM project types can be aggregated from a set of 17 reusable method fragments.
- Situated: Generality level is "one of a kind", i.e. the method is applicable only in a specific organization for a specific process at a specific point in time. Aggregation level is "specific technique", i. e. only selected BPM aspects are covered. BPM methods (or better approaches) on this level of abstraction are either individually developed 'on the fly', or are instantiated from more abstract methods.

Theoretically, artifacts of every type can be represented on a literally unlimited number of abstraction levels. The generality and aggregation levels of constructs, descriptive models, problem or solution models, or solution methods are implied by specifying the respective scope or problem class, e. g. by focusing on design goals, application areas, problem characteristics, etc. In order to discover relevant focus dimensions, an empirical technique like the one proposed by Winter [30] can be used. By using principal component analysis on data of 47 BPM projects, Winter yielded four relevant focus dimensions for BPM: performance measurement maturity, process orientation maturity, process manager impact, and methodology and standard maturity [29]. By choosing more or less restrictive ranges for these four focus dimensions, a BPM problem class is defined for which respective descriptive or solution artifacts can be constructed. If every observed BPM approach in a company is represented in the four dimensional room spanned by the four discovered focus dimensions, a cluster analysis can be carried out to determine a reasonable number of clusters, i. e. design problem classes. The higher number of clusters is chosen, the larger the set of problem classes will be, and the less abstract will be respective descriptive and solution artifacts. Fig. 3 is a typical dendrogram-like tree diagram that results from agglomerative clustering and illustrates how artifacts on different abstraction levels are related.

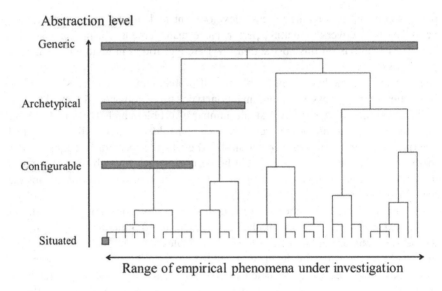

Fig. 3. Ultrametric tree visualization of artifact generality [adapted from 31]

The vertical dimension in Fig. 3 can be illustrated by characterizing four exemplary levels of abstraction of an solution model: The situated artifact's scope is limited to exactly one empirical phenomenon, e. g. a solution instance in a specific organization at a specific point in time. The configurable artifact's scope covers a certain range of phenomena delimited by a reusable set of description or solution components, e. g. a certain type of decision problems that can be solved by a parameterized algorithm. The archetypal artifact's scope covers a larger range of phenomena defined by a problem class context and certain analysis / design goals, e. g. BPM in large discrete manufacturing companies. The generic artifact's scope is the largest, covering an entire class of phenomena, e. g. performance management in commercial organizations. The (dis)similarity of two artifacts corresponds to the generality level of their link. If two artifacts are very similar, their link is represented on a low level of generality – and vice versa.

2.3   Four Artifact 'Worlds'

We have argued that artifacts can be differentiated regarding whether (1) they are descriptive or prescriptive and (2) regarding their level of abstraction – which can be expressed by their degree of aggregation and generalization. Since these two dimensions are sufficiently independent, their combination yields four different artifact 'worlds':

1. The *world of explanations* (quadrant E in Fig. 4) is the quadrant where artifact use is analyzed, explained and/or predicted on a general level. The most important artifacts in this quadrant are descriptive models including their conceptual base (construct definitions). An example for E-artifacts is the Technology Acceptance Model which explains/predicts IS acceptance by end users through (a) reconstruction of constructs like 'intention to use' or 'IS acceptance' and (b) empirical validation of a hypothetical dependency between these constructs that can be interpreted as causality ('acceptance of x by y is dependent to extent z on intention of y to use x'). E-artifacts are primarily created by descriptive research using social science techniques. Validity is the most desirable property of descriptive models. Among equally valid E-artifacts, those are usually higher valued that are more general and / or more comprehensive.

2. The *world of technologies* (quadrant T in Fig. 4) is the quadrant where solution models are related to problem models. The most important artifacts in this quadrant are design theories which, e. g. in the form of 'technological rules' or patterns or methods, link solution components (i. e. components of solution models or solution activities) to requirements (i. e. components of problem models). An example for T-artifacts is Activity Based Costing, a means to enable an organization to make appropriate (e. g. pricing, order acceptance) decisions in the presence of complex service processes, unsteady capacity usage and large indirect costs. T-artifacts are primarily created by problem-solving research using engineering techniques. Researchers might take an observer role, but can also be directly involved into solution design (action design research [32]). 'Effectiveness' is the most desirable property of technologies. Among equally effective T-artifacts, those are usually higher valued that are more general and / or more comprehensive.

3. The *world of solutions* (quadrant S in Fig. 4) is the quadrant where specific organizational design problems are addressed (and hopefully solved) by suitable artifacts. In contrast to quadrant T, such artifacts are not abstract any more, but adapted, configured/composed and/or implemented for solving a specific problem of a specific organization at a specific point in time – yet not implemented. The content of this quadrant can be characterized as '(concrete) problem solution' with specific problem-solving power being its most desirable property. Examples of S-artifacts are concrete process workflows to handle a business transaction (= instantiated process models) or concrete project plans (= instantiated solution methods) to achieve a business goal. S-artifacts are created in practice.

4. The *world of operations* (quadrant O in Fig. 4) is the quadrant where artifact application and use are described on an instance level. In contrast to quadrant S which covers constructed artifacts, implemented O-artifacts are 'in action'. In contrast to quadrant E, artifact use and its consequences are described individually on an instance level and not generalized. The content of this quadrant can be characterized as concrete day-to-day operations of organizations, with performance relative to the respective business goals being its most desirable property. Examples of O-artifacts are descriptions of the actual handling of a business transaction or the actual execution of a project. O-artifacts are created in practice.

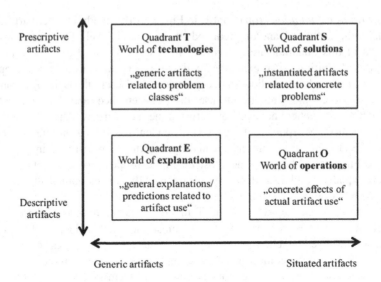

Fig. 4. Artifact 'worlds' quadrant model

3　Theory Building and Theory Application Activities

The four-world model is providing one common reference frame for representing abstract descriptive knowledge (quadrant E, e. g. explanatory theories), generalized solution knowledge (quadrant T, e. g. solution methods and solution models), concrete descriptive knowledge (quadrant O, e. g. observations of actual IS use) and concrete solutions (quadrant S, e. g. concrete workflows and plans). A common framework should however not only allow integrating all relevant artifact types, but also all activities and processes that create and use such artifacts. In the following, we therefore characterize 'intra-world' and 'inter-world' activities based on the proposed quadrant model and link the findings with existing reference process models from DSR-IS.

The most obvious activities are those that use and create artifacts within a world:

1. Within quadrant E, the body of (analytical / explanatory / predictive) theory knowledge can always be extended by combining or refining theories. Without data input from quadrant O (e.g. observations of innovative practices), new aspects of the phenomenon cannot be theorized. As a consequence, the significance of processes within quadrant O is limited to incremental progress.

2. Within quadrant T, the body of technologies can be extended by combining or refining problem / solution models or solution methods. Without input from quadrant S (e.g. analyzing novel solutions from practice) or quadrant E (e.g. applying new justificatory theory), however, the significance of processes within quadrant T is also limited to incremental progress (like e.g. improved modularization of a method).

3. Within quadrant S, the body of artifact instantiations can be extended by combining or refining solutions, or by applying existing technologies to new problems. Without input from quadrant T (e.g. new technologies) or quadrant O (e.g. observations of innovative practices), however, neither alternative, hopefully more effective solutions for existing problems can be found, nor can empirical evidence be used to enhance the effectiveness of solutions. A significant source of novel artifacts can however result from innovative solutions that have not been instantiated from existing technologies, but applied an invention outside our model, e. g. a new information technology or a new idea for structuring a task. It might also be possible to identify novel technologies but search.

4. Within quadrant O, the amount of knowledge about artifact implementation can be extended by collecting additional observations from the real world.

Hence the most important intra-world activities seem to be found in T (non-evidence-based solution innovation) and in O (exploration of innovative practices).

In a next step, we characterize activities that connect different worlds:

- From operations to explanations: Theory building is the process of generalizing observations (O-artifacts) in order to add generic descriptive analyses / explanations / predictions to the world of explanations, i. e. to create new E-artifacts from O-artifacts. An example is to collect a large number of actual IS acceptance observations in order to validate a general hypothesis about IS acceptance. We designate this activity O⇒E as it connects quadrant O to quadrant E.

- From explanations to technologies: DSR-IS nis the process of creating innovative, generic problem solutions (T-artifacts) that can be added to the world of technologies, ideally based on general descriptive analyses / explanations / prescriptions from the world of explanations (E-artifacts). This process is not a mere transformation, but requires to specify design goals, differentiate design situations, validate effectiveness / utility claims, etc. An example is to transform the Technology Acceptance Model into design guidelines for IS that avoid certain acceptance problems. We designate this activity E⇒T as is connects quadrant E to quadrant T.

- From technologies to solutions: Solution engineering means to situate, adapt, instantiate and maybe extend generic solutions from the world of technologies (T-artifacts) to create or improve concrete solutions to concrete design problems (S-artifacts). An example is to identify, prioritize and apply certain design principles, to identify and instantiate solution methods and/or to identify and adapt reference solution models in IS development. We designate this activity T⇒S as is connects quadrant T to quadrant S.

- From solutions to operations: Implementation / introduction means to put concrete project plans, concrete enterprise models (S-artifacts) etc. in action in a specific organization at a specific point in time to solve a specific problem (i. e. to create O-artifacts). An example is to run a project, to implement an IS or to execute a process. We designate this activity S⇒O as is connects quadrant S to quadrant O.

The above mentioned activities are illustrated based on the proposed artifact framework in Fig. 5.

When linked together, E⇒T, T⇒S and S⇒O can be interpreted as 'evidence-based' design. Similar to evidence-based medicine or evidence-based management [33], this means that solutions are systematically based on justificatory knowledge (cause-effect relations) as well as applicable technologies (means-end relations) – in contrast to purely 'search-based' design [e.g. 34].

O⇒E (theory building, the core activity of descriptive research) is the 'missing link' to complete a process cycle within the proposed framework. The resulting research process might start with making real-world observations (O), finding explanations (O⇒E), transforming these into innovative technologies (E⇒T), apply such innovations to real-world problems (T⇒S), implement these solutions (S⇒O), and finally evaluate how they perform in order to extend/revise explanations (O⇒E), enhance technologies (E⇒T), and so on. This chain of processes comes very close to a combination of widely accepted process models for DSR-IS (e.g. [35]) with the classical process of theory-building in social sciences (e.g. [23]).

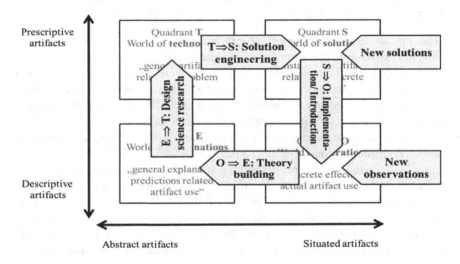

Fig. 5. Theory building and theory application in the proposed artifact framework

Our first research question aimed at integrating descriptive and design research activities. If O⇒E represents descriptive research and (E⇒T; T⇒S; S⇒O) represents design research, the proposed framework provides a conceptual foundation for connecting DSR-IS to theory-building in information systems research.

4   De-contextualization and Emergence

Does the 'intertwining' of theory building with DSR-IS only work in a 'forward-engineering', evidence-based way? Can innovative solutions only be created by situating, adapting, instantiating and maybe extending general technologies that rely on justificatory foundations – that themselves have been validated by observing existing phenomena? How can innovation be explained when there is no innovative design without justificatory explanations, and when explanations rely on observations of 'applied theory'?

An alternative understanding of design has been proposed by van Aken and others who endorse inductive design by empirical research on multiple case studies to determine existing best practice. E. g., van Aken and Nagel [36] use seven case studies to identify technological rules which solve the problems associated with the 'fuzzy front end' of the product development process. As Davies [37] summarizes this approach, "once a rule has been identified, it is then tested in a range of contexts, with adjustments being made when needed, until 'theoretical saturation' is reached and additional cases do not add anything to knowledge about when and how the rule works".

The induction of 'technologies' (i.e. means-end relations) has also been proposed under the 'pattern' label not only in civil engineering [e.g. 10] or software engineering [e.g. 11], but also in the context of organizational design and engineering [see e.g. 12, 13]. The apparent benefit of inductive design is that yet 'unexplained', innovative practices can be generalized and reused without have to take the 'detour' of descriptive theorizing. It is however unclear how inductive design should be structured from a conceptual research process perspective and which components of inductive design can be integrated with evidence-based design or with descriptive research activities.

The question is whether an inductive identification of technologies is compatible with DSR-IS. For strategies that have not been formulated and implemented (Mintzberg and Waters use the term 'designed') deliberately, but instead become evident as "a pattern in a stream of decisions" (i.e. are implied by their implementation only), Mintzberg and Waters [38] coined the attribute 'emergent'. Van Burg et al. [39] apply the distinction between deliberate and emergent design to organized systems:

- *Deliberate Design*: (Descriptive) research findings (E-artifacts) are used to identify design principles (T-artifacts) which are used to construct design solutions (S-artifacts) which are in turn implemented as practices (O-artifacts) which might allow new/better research findings. Van Burg et al. [39] designate this as "a process of contextualization". It corresponds to evidence-based design as characterized above.
- *Emergent Design*: Innovative practices (O-artifacts) are generalized as design solutions (S-artifacts) which allow to infer design principles (T-artifacts) which in turn allow to infer research findings (E-artifacts). Van Burg et al. [39] designate this as "a process of de-contextualization". This process has not yet been positioned in the framework proposed here.

4.1   'Backward' Design Activities

In the light of Van Burg et al.'s [39] proposal, the evidence-based design process proposed in the preceding section is 'deliberate': $E{\Rightarrow}T$, $T{\Rightarrow}S$ and $S{\Rightarrow}O$ move not only upward in the Chmielewicz pyramid (theory$\Rightarrow$model/method$\Rightarrow$instantiation), but also decrease abstraction so that this process chain is 'a process of contextualization'. Can the proposed four quadrant model also be used as a foundation to illustrate de-contextualization processes in IS-DSR?

- Concrete problem solutions (S) need often be repeatedly revised or extended based on insights from their actual use (or not-use) in the world of operations (O).

An example is the revision of an IS solution to overcome user resistance that results from a not easy-to-use interface or from functional deficits. We designate this process as O⇒S as it connects quadrant O to quadrant S.

- Generic artifacts (T) need also often to be repeatedly revised or extended based on insights from applying them in the world of solutions (S). An example is the revision of a design theory to cover contexts or problem aspects that were not covered before and that become apparent during instantiation. We designate this process as S⇒T as it connects quadrant S to quadrant T.
- Finally, generic explanations (E) need sometimes to be revised or extended based on insights from trying to use them for problem-solving (as kernel theories for designing technologies T). An example is the extension of IS use theories by social networking aspects because observed technology adoption effects in the presence of social networking seems to call for new / amended explanations. We designate this process as T⇒E as it connects quadrant T to quadrant E.

When linked together, O⇒S and S⇒T form the backward (feedback) component of the build cycle, the core cycle of design science research [40]. This is illustrated by Figure 6.

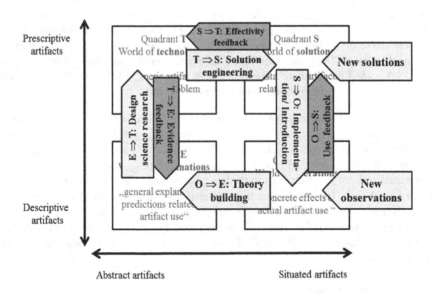

Fig. 6. The 'build cycle'

The backward / feedback process is however not emergent, but rather a necessary component of deliberate design – and a consequence of the understanding of IS-DSR as a directed search process [34]. The same hold for T⇒E which is also has more the character of a feedback mechanism (of deliberate theory-building) than that of 'emergent theory-building'.

4.2   Emergent Design

The question is therefore whether really 'emergent', de-contextualization processes can be included in the proposed framework. To that end, we characterize inductive design activities in the following:

- Solution induction: By aggregating use data over several time periods, users, use situations, or even organizational sub-structures, solution use data (O-artifacts) can be de-contextualized into solution knowledge (S-artifacts). E. g., configuration options of a concrete IS solution can be inferred by collecting data about what actual functions are used by what types of users in what use situation [41]. We designate this de-contextualization activity as O⇒SE.
- Technology induction: By pattern recognition, classification or techniques like Quantitative Case Analysis [42], technologies (T-artifacts) can be inferred from innovative concrete problem solutions (S-artifacts). Examples are the inductive design of a reference process model from observed 'best practice' processes, the inductive design of a maturity model from observed successful capability improvement practices, or the inductive design of a method from observed successful procedures. Depending on the desired degree of de-contextualization, various levels of generality can be realized (see sub-section on artifact generality above and examples in [30]). We designate this de-contextualization activity as S⇒TE.

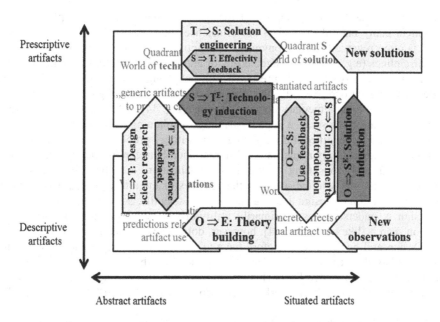

Fig. 7. Evidence-based and inductive design

Fig. 7 adds solution and technology induction to the evidence-based design activities to the already positioned build cycle and theory-building activities. This extension addresses our second research question, the inclusion of inductive design activities.

4.3   Design and Engineering Iterations

The proposed conceptualization of ODE artifacts and processes not only allows representing elementary activities, contextualization, de-contextualization and emergence processes. Furthermore, commonly found activity patterns can be represented as partial cycles:

- Iterations of S⇒O and O⇒S represent 'instance improvement': Implementation/use feedback is used to improve a solution without being reflected by enhancing generic technology design.
- Iterations of T⇒S and S⇒T around (S⇒O)(O⇒S) iterations represent 'theory-agnostic design': The process is a sequence of build-and-evaluate cycles which are however not explicitly founded on analytical / explanatory / prescriptive models, i.e. do not sufficiently consider (and of course not enhance) the descriptive knowledge base.
- Iterations of E⇒T and T⇒E around (T⇒S)(S⇒T) cycles represent evidence-based IS-DSR because the build-and-evaluate cycles are based on kernel theories and might contribute to their enhancement by "learning and theorizing" [43].

5   Conclusions

Based on the traditional dominance of the quest for describing and explaining the present in many natural as well as social sciences (e.g. physics or sociology), 'science' is often regarded as a synonym for descriptive research. For many other scientific disciplines (e.g. medicine, engineering, or architecture), the dominant quest is not understanding or explaining the present world, but changing the current world into a better or preferred one. Nevertheless, this quest is often not designated as 'science', but instead as a complementary concept 'design' [e.g. 44] or 'engineering' [e.g. 45]. The differentiation of 'science = understanding / explaining / predicting' on the one hand, and 'design / engineering = creating / innovating / problem solving' on the other, however, might imply a qualitative differentiation between 'research' activities on the one hand, and 'consulting', 'clinical' or 'application' activities on the other. In this regard, Simon's seminal work on the sciences of the artificial [34] was a much needed recognition of design and engineering as a scientific activity [e.g. 46]. As long as design is understood as a primarily utility-driven, not necessarily theory-based solution search [like e.g. in 16, 34], however, doubts on its scientific nature will persist. Design and engineering therefore have to develop from 'experience-based' into 'evidence-based' activities, i. e. need to be founded on the available body of theory and technology knowledge [46]. This requirement was the starting point for our proposal of an integrative framework for descriptive and 'designed' (or 'engineered') research artifacts.

While the core product of descriptive research is a (generalized) descriptive model, the core product of DSR is a "well-tested solution concept, i.e. a generic intervention to solve a generic field problem, tested in the laboratory and in the field of its intended use." [46] These artifacts are both abstract, i.e. apply to a large number of individual observations or solutions, respectively. If we add (individual) observations as empirical base of theory building and (individual) solutions as instantiations of generalized interventions (= technologies) to the generic artifacts, we yield the core objects of the proposed four world quadrant model. Such a framework not only helps to better characterize the nature, and identify synergies, between research activities, but also to organize the vast theory and technology knowledge base of organizational design and engineering in a way that supports reuse and integration better. An application for IS-DSR can found e.g. in [47].

Since innovation is not always based on descriptive theory and technology advancements (as well as proper solution engineering and implementation), but can also be enabled by exogenous solution innovation or observed novel practices, inductive research activities need to be integrated with traditional, evidence-based activities. We therefore included not only forward-engineering and feedback activities, but also induction activities into our analysis.

In addition to improving the systematization, access and reuse of knowledge on observations, theories, technologies and solutions in IS-DSR, we see the following challenges that require further research:

- *Understanding Abstraction*: While the semantic boundary between descriptive artifacts (related to empirical facts) and prescriptive artifacts (related to goals and contexts) clearly structures the vertical dimension of the framework, the horizontal dimension is complex, even within a single problem domain. Both the design of generalized solutions as well as the classification / abstraction of concrete practices / operations / decisions rely on a clear and common understanding of abstraction levels, construct clustering, configuration rules, etc. Compared to extreme artifact situation (e.g., cases) and to extreme artifact abstraction ("one size fits all" concepts), this sub-field of IS-DSR appears to be underrepresented and needs more attention.

- *Understanding Use and Context:* Theoretically, the grounding of means-end relations on appropriate cause-effect relations is straightforward: if the ends correspond to a desired effect, then the means is to realize the cause. In real-life design and engineering, however, 'realizing' or 'implementing' causes or linking design goals to theoretical effects is not so straightforward, in particular if use and context are important factors to consider or if explanatory factors and design factors differ. While in organizational sciences it has been proposed to extend 'technological rules' by including context and intervention [48], in IS-DSR multi-grounding [19] or the use of testable design product / process hypotheses [5] has been advocated. A thorough conceptual analysis would certainly help to bring more light into this issue. A unified model of (organizational) context would be a good starting point.

- *Different Disciplinary Culture:* A better integration of design-oriented research with descriptive research requires not only a common framework (that provides common object, dependency and activity definitions, maybe even a common understanding of context and use), but also some compatibility of competencies and disciplinary culture. The boundary between validity (as primary research goal in the descriptive realm) and utility (as primary research goal in the design realm) has fundamental consequences e. g. for evaluation processes, the role perception of researchers, or the closeness of the respective research community to practice. With a common foundation in place, organizing research knowledge accordingly might be a starting point. The mindset barriers between understanding the world and creating a better world will however always limit the synergy potentials between these research communities.

- *Systematic Discovery:* Finally, this proposal puts emphasis on the concept of de-contextualization and inductive design. Discovery-oriented activities provide an additional path (complementary to the evidence-based path) from detecting innovative practices to better solutions and better technologies / designs. Inductive design has only rarely addressed so far. We believe that a combination of inductive and deductive design activities has a great potential because innovations are often not driven by academia, but by corporate decision makers, solution vendors and consultants in the real world, so that systematic discovery mechanisms would definitely support research that is not only rigorous, but also relevant. This would however require paying more academic attention to solution induction and technology induction.

References

1. Winter, R.: A Framework for Evidence-based and Inductive Design. In: Magalhaes, R. (ed.) Organization Design and Engineering: Co-Existence, Cooperation or Integration? (to appear 2014)
2. Gregor, S.: The Nature of Theory in Information Systems. MIS Quarterly 30(3), 611–642 (2006)
3. Bhattacherjee, A.: Understanding Information Systems Continuance: An Expectation-Confirmation Model. MIS Quarterly 25(3), 351–370 (2001)
4. Baskerville, R.L., Pries-Heje, J.: Explanatory Design Theory. Business & Information Systems Engineering 2(5), 271–282 (2010)
5. Walls, J.G., Widmeyer, G.R., El Sawy, O.A.: Building an Information System Design Theory for Vigilant EIS. Information Systems Research 3(1), 36–59 (1992)
6. Winter, R.: Design Science Research in Europe. European Journal of Information Systems 17(5), 470–475 (2008)
7. Österle, H., Becker, J., Frank, U., Hess, T., Karagiannis, D., Krcmar, H., Loos, P., Mertens, P., Oberweis, A., Sinz, E.: Memorandum on design-oriented information systems research. European Journal of Information Systems 20(1), 7–10 (2011)
8. Junglas, I., Niehaves, B., Spiekermann, S., Stahl, B.C., Weitzel, T., Winter, R., Baskerville, R.L.: The inflation of academic intellectual capital: the case for design science research in Europe. European Journal of Information Systems 20(1), 1–6 (2011)
9. Gregor, S., Jones, D.: The Anatomy of a Design Theory. Journal of the Association for Information Systems 8(5), 312–335 (2007)
10. Alexander, C., Ishikawa, S., Silverstein, M., Jacobson, M., Fiksdahl-King, I., Angel, S.: A Pattern Language. Oxford University Press (1977)
11. Gamma, E., Helm, R., Johnson, R., Vlissides, J.: Design Patterns: Elements of Reusable Object-Oriented Software. Addison-Wesley, Reading (1995)
12. Mintzberg, H.: Patterns in strategy formation. Management Science 24(9), 934–948 (1978)
13. Mettler, T., Eurich, M.: What is the business model behind e-health? A pattern-based approach to sustainable profit. In: Proceedings of 20th European Conference on Information Systems, Barcelona, Spain (2012)

14. March, S.T., Smith, G.F.: Design and Natural Science Research on Information Technology. Decision Support Systems 15(4), 251–266 (1995)
15. Vahidov, R.: Design Researcher's IS Artifact - A Representational Framework. In: Proc. DESRIST 2006, Claremont, pp. 19–33 (2006)
16. Hevner, A.R., March, S.T., Park, J., Ram, S.: Design Science in Information Systems Research. MIS Quarterly 28(1), 75–105 (2004)
17. Chmielewicz, K.: Forschungskonzeptionen der Wirtschaftswissenschaften, 3 ed, 3rd edn. Poeschel, Stuttgart (1994)
18. Gericke,   A.:   Konstruktionsforschung   und   Artefaktkonstruktion   in   der gestaltungsorientierten Wirtschaftsinformatik: Ein Literaturüberblick, Research Report, Institute of Information Management, University of St. Gallen (2008)
19. Goldkuhl, G.: Design Theories in Information Systems - A Need for Multi-Grounding. Journal of Information Technology Theory and Application 6(2), 59–72 (2004)
20. Venable, J.R.: The Role of Theory and Theorising in Design Science Research. In: Proceedings DESRIST 2006, Claremont, pp. 1–18 (2006)
21. Winter, R., Gericke, A., Bucher, T.: Method Versus Model – Two Sides of the Same Coin? In: Albani, A., Barjis, J., Dietz, J.L.G. (eds.) CIAO! 2009. LNBIP, vol. 34, pp. 1–15. Springer, Heidelberg (2009)
22. van de Weerd, I., de Weerd, S., Brinkkemper, S.: Developing a Reference Method for Game Production by Method Comparison. In: Ralyté, J., Brinkkemper, S., Henderson-Sellers, B. (eds.) Situational Method Engineering: Fundamentals and Experiences. IFIP, vol. 244, pp. 313–327. Springer, Heidelberg (2007)
23. Kerlinger, F.N.: Foundations of Behavioral Research; Educational and Psychological Inquiry. Holt Rinehart and Winston, New York (1964)
24. Iivari, J.: A Paradigmatic Analysis of Information Systems As a Design Science. Scandinavian Journal of Information Systems 19(2) (2007)
25. Gehlert, A., Schermann, M., Pohl, K., Krcmar, H.: Towards a research method for theory driven design research. In: Proceedings of Wirtschaftsinformatik, pp. 441–450 (2009)
26. Smith, J.M., Smith, D.C.P.: Database abstractions: aggregation and generalization. ACM Transactions on Database Systems (TODS) 2(2), 105–133 (1977)
27. Malone, T.W., Crowston, K., Lee, J., Pentland, B.T., Dellarocas, C., Wyner, G.M., Quimby, J., Osborn, C.S., Bernstein, A., Herman, G.A., et al.: Tools for Inventing Organizations: Toward a Handbook of Organizational Processes. Management Science 45(3), 425–443 (1999)
28. Bucher, T., Winter, R.: Project Types of Business Process Management – Towards a Scenario Structure to Enable Situational Method Engineering for Business Process Management. Business Process Management Journal 15(4), 548–568 (2009)
29. Bucher, T., Winter, R.: Taxonomy of Business Process Management Approaches: An Empirical Foundation for the Engineering of Situational Methods to Support BPM. In: vom Brocke, J., Rosemann, M. (eds.) Handbook on Business Process Management, vol. 2, pp. 93–114. Springer, Heidelberg (2010)
30. Winter, R.: Construction of Situational Information Systems Management Methods. International Journal of Information System Modeling and Design 3(4), 67–85 (2012)
31. Winter, R.: Problem Analysis for Situational Artefact Construction in Information Systems in Andrea Carugati and Cecilia Rossignoli, ed. In: Emerging Themes in Information Systems and Organization Studies, pp. 97–113. Physica, Heidelberg (2011)
32. Sein, M., Henfridsson, O., Purao, S., Rossi, M., Lindgren, R.: Action Design Research. MIS Quarterly 35(1), 37–56 (2011)

33. Rousseau, D.M.: The Oxford Handbook of Evidence-based Management. Oxford University Press, New York (2012)
34. Simon, H.A.: The Sciences of the Artificial, vol. 3. MIT Press, Cambridge (1996)
35. Peffers, K., Tuunanen, T., Rothenberger, M., Chatterjee, S.: A Design Science Research Methodology for Information Systems Research. Journal of Management Information Systems 24(3), 45–77 (2007)
36. van Aken, J.E., Nagel, A.P.: Organising and managing the fuzzy front end of new product development, Research Report, Technical University Eindhoven (2004)
37. Davies, H.: Improving the Relevance of Management Research: Evidence-Based Management: Design Science or Both? Business Leadership Review (July 2006)
38. Mintzberg, H., Waters, J.A.: Of strategies, deliberate and emergent. Strategic Management Journal 6(3), 257–272 (1985)
39. Van Burg, E., Romme, A.G.L., Reymen, I.M.M.J., Gilsing, V.A.: Creating University Spinoffs: A Science-Based Design Perspective. Journal of Product Innovation Management 25(2), 114–128 (2008)
40. Hevner, A.R.: A Three Cycle View of Design Science Research. Scandinavian Journal of Information Systems 19(2), 87–92 (2007)
41. Mayer, J.H., Bischoff, S., Winter, R., Weitzel, T.: Extending Traditional EIS Use to Support Mobile Executives Online and Offline. MIS Quarterly Executive 22(2), 87–96 (2012)
42. Ragin, C.C.: Set Relations in Social Research: Evaluating Their Consistency and Coverage. Political Analysis, 291–310 (2006)
43. Rossi, M., Sein, M.K.: Design Research Workshop: A Proactive Research Approach. In: Proc. IRIS 2003. IRIS Association (2003)
44. Romme, A.G.L.: Making a Differnce: Organization as Design. Organization Science 14(5), 558–573 (2003)
45. Magalhaes, R., Silva, A.R.: Organizational Design and Engineering (ODE), Research Report, Technical University of Lisbon (2009)
46. van Aken, J.E., Romme, A.G.L.: A Design Science Approach to Evidence-based Management in Denise. In: Rousseau, M. (ed.) The Oxford Handbook of Evidence-based Management, Oxford University Press, New York (2012)
47. Winter, R., Albani, A.: Restructuring the Design Science Research Knowledge Base - A One-Cycle View of Design Science Research and its Consequences for Understanding Organizational Design Problems in Richard Baskerville. In: Baskerville, R., de Marco, M., Spagnoletti, P. (eds.) Designing Organizational Systems: An Interdisciplinary Discourse, pp. 63–81. Springer, Heidelberg (2013)
48. Denyer, D., Tranfield, D., van Aken, J.E.: Developing Design Propositions through Research Synthesis. Organization Studies 29, 393–413 (2008)

Design Science and Innovation Practices: A Delphi Study

Alan R. Hevner[1] and Jack Anderson[2]

[1] University of South Florida
ahevner@usf.edu
[2] Chevron Corporation, San Ramon, CA, USA
jack.anderson@chevron.com

Abstract. Current innovation practice demonstrates many of the ideas of design thinking. In this paper, we explore the readiness of innovation practice to include design science concepts and processes. At a recent conference, an initial round of a Delphi study engaged a number of innovation practitioners in a discussion around the question, "Is design science the future of innovation?" The results of the study are presented as summaries of opportunities and challenges in bringing design science into innovation practice.

Keywords: Design Science Research, Innovation, Delphi Study.

1   Introduction

Innovation: (Merriam-Webster Dictionary)
- *(noun) A new idea, device, or method*
- *(verb) The act or process of introducing new ideas, devices, or methods*

The territory covered by the term *innovation* is immense. The human actors in this landscape are many and varied, including managers, inventors, creative employees, entrepreneurs, university researchers, government funders, and policy makers among many others. All players concede that innovation is of vital importance to organizations, economies, and to society as a whole. "Virtually all of the economic growth that has occurred since the eighteenth century is ultimately attributable to innovation" (Baumol 2002). Innovative activities are strongly linked to business performance in industry leaders such as Apple, Google, and Adidas (Innovaro 2008).

We see many different perspectives when viewing innovation and innovation success. Industry managers expect innovation success to result in greater market share and higher levels of profitability from resulting products and services. Governmental research funding bodies expect that external societal impacts from publicly funded research should be assessed, as in the United Kingdom's Research Excellence Framework[1] and the United States National Science Foundation's Merit Review

---

[1] http://www.ref.ac.uk/

M. Helfert et al. (Eds.): EDSS 2013, CCIS 447, pp. 21–27, 2014.

Criteria[2]. Academic researchers are interested in innovative activity as it leads to new knowledge contributions in traditional outlets such as archival journals. In sum, the current innovation landscape has many disparate players with different goals and different understandings and measures of innovation effectiveness and success.

In this short paper, we explore the existing gap between innovation practice in industry centered on design thinking and leading-edge innovation research in academia centered on design science. A preliminary Delphi study is performed with industry innovation practitioners around the question, "Is design science the future of innovation?" The results of the study are presented as summaries of opportunities and challenges in bringing design science into the practice of innovation.

2   Innovation Practice and Design Thinking

Our premise for this research is that the current practices of innovation make use of the best ideas of design thinking. Design thinking, as described by Cross (2011), is a formal method for the practical, creative resolution of problems or opportunities with the intent of an improved result. It is a form of solution-focused thinking which starts with a goal and using a design process builds an innovative artifact that can be evaluated for evidence of a better future situation. The essence of design thinking can be found in most, if not all of the successful innovation practices found in industry, including the popular IDEO innovation methods (Kelley and Littman 2001).

As one of the co-authors has spent many years in industry working with innovation teams and holds the position of innovation leader for a large corporation, we propose to make the following observations on the current state of innovation practice:

- Innovation practitioners desire the ability to understand, measure, and improve their innovation processes.
- Current innovation methods are largely ad-hoc, non-directed activities in most organizations (e.g. free time to explore new and different opportunities).
- A few organizations are recognized for innovation excellence but it is difficult to capture their successful activities into a generalized set of methods for all organizations and contexts.
- In general, there are no unifying structures, practices, nor common vocabulary for innovation practices that pervade industry, government, or academia.

Based on these observations, we claim that the ideas of design thinking are the unstated unifier of innovation practice across industry. We contend that effective organizations leverage and enact design thinking in their innovation practices without full awareness of design thinking as an informing methodology. We also find no organizations that claim to employ innovation methods that fall outside the scope of design thinking.

Thus, given the current design thinking basis for industrial innovation practices, we look to the next wave of innovation processes and ask, "Is design science the future of innovation?" After a brief digression to define design science, we explore this question with a preliminary Delphi study.

---

[2] http://www.nsf.gov/bfa/dias/policy/merit_review/

3   Design Science Research

The design science research (DSR) paradigm has its roots in engineering and the sciences of the artificial (Simon 1996). It is fundamentally a problem-solving paradigm. In the field of information and computer technology (ICT), design science seeks to create innovations that define the ideas, practices, technical capabilities, and products through which the analysis, design, implementation, and use of information systems (IS) can be effectively and efficiently accomplished. The activities of DSR within the IS discipline are described via a conceptual framework and a set of seven guidelines for conducting and evaluating good design science research in (Hevner et al. 2004). Formal and rigorous adherence to the seven guidelines as shown in Table 1 is a clear distinction between design thinking and design science.

Table 1. Design Science Research Guidelines

Guideline	Description
Guideline 1: Design as an Artifact	Design-science research must produce a viable artifact in the form of a construct, a model, a method, or an instantiation.
Guideline 2: Problem Relevance	The objective of design-science research is to develop technology-based solutions to important and relevant business problems.
Guideline 3: Design Evaluation	The utility, quality, and efficacy of a design artifact must be rigorously demonstrated via well-executed evaluation methods.
Guideline 4: Research Contributions	Effective design-science research must provide clear and verifiable contributions in the areas of the design artifact, design foundations, and/or design methodologies.
Guideline 5: Research Rigor	Design-science research relies upon the application of rigorous methods in both the construction and evaluation of the design artifact.
Guideline 6: Design as a Search Process	The search for an effective artifact requires utilizing available means to reach desired ends while satisfying laws in the problem environment.
Guideline 7: Communication of Research	Design-science research must be presented effectively both to technology-oriented as well as management-oriented audiences.

In particular, it is important to highlight guideline 4. DSR must provide contributions to both the application environment in the form of a problem-solving artifact and an addition to the field's knowledge base. Contributions to scientific knowledge will include any extensions to the original theories and methods made during the research, the new artifacts (design products and processes), and all experiences gained from performing the iterative design cycles and field testing of the artifact in the application environment. It is imperative that a design science innovation project makes a compelling case for its rigorous bases and contributions lest the research be dismissed as a case of routine design.

In prior stages of our research project, we investigated how design science methods can be applied to innovation practice. In Anderson et al. (2011), we used a real-life case study of an IDEO-based Innovation Cycle in Chevron to perform a gap-analysis with design science. The results of the study suggested that there are key insights that can be drawn from the design science concepts and guidelines that can potentially impact and improve organizational innovation processes. Based on these insights, in Hevner et al. (2012) we proposed a DSR-influenced innovation model termed DRIVES (Design Research for Innovation Value, Evaluation, and Sustainability). This six-stage model incorporates process steps for the discovery and development of innovative artifacts that satisfies the DSR guidelines. The next research stage reported here is to gauge the reaction of innovation practitioners to the design science concepts.

4   A Delphi Study

4.1   Innovation Conference Setting

To address the question of whether innovation practitioners view design science as a promising next wave for innovation methods, we participated in the 4th Annual Process Driven Innovation Conference[3] held September 17-18, 2013 in Philadelphia. The conference purpose was stated as: "Bring together senior level executives in product development to discuss their innovation processes as well as the latest product development technologies. Furthermore, attendees will analyze groundbreaking methodologies to effectively manage a multi-tiered process innovation portfolio, cultivate a culture that embraces risk and creativity, and generate metrics to monitor the effectiveness, efficiency, and viability of initiatives across the process innovation pipeline."

During the conference sessions, over 20 well-known companies gave in-depth presentations about their newest and most effective innovation practices. Our informal analysis of these presentations identified a large majority of these best innovation practices involved ideas central to design thinking. We also found a small subset of the presentations referring to ideas that we would consider beyond design thinking and approaching the ideas of design science.

4.2   The Delphi Method

During the innovation conference we arranged and structured several occasions to interact with small subsets of attendees to solicit their opinions on the future of innovation practices and the potentials of design science ideas in that future. We structured these interactions in the form of the first round of a Delphi Method study.

---

[3] http://www.marcusevans-conferences-PDI

The Delphi Method is a structured communication technique used to investigate a complex problem (Linstone and Turoff 1975). Panels of experts are engaged in multiple rounds of inquiry. After each round, a summary of the expert opinions is produced and the problem is re-defined for the next round. The goal is that during the process the range of solutions will decrease and the Delphi method will converge toward the 'correct' or a 'satisfactory' answer to the problem. The process is completed based on pre-defined stopping criteria (e.g. number of rounds, solution consensus, or stability of results).

4.3   Data Gathering Opportunities

The conference was attended by 97 innovation practitioners from over 50 different organizations. One of the co-authors gave a short plenary address to all attendees covering an overview of design science concepts. Thus, there was a minimal awareness of design science by everyone who was paying attention. No opportunity for feedback was available in this session.

A half-day workshop presented by both co-authors on DSR and its application to innovation was held with an attendance of eight individuals representing seven organizations. After a fuller overview of design science ideas, the attendees were engaged in a structured round of questioning using Delphi methods of data gathering.

On the final day of the conference, we arranged a luncheon discussion on design science and innovation that attracted 15 attendees. In this constrained setting we provided a brief discussion of the relationship of design science and innovation. Afterwards, we were able to engage this group also in an abbreviated round of questioning using the Delphi method.

In sum, we were able to capture qualitative, descriptive data from 18 participants based on responses and discussions on structured questions addressing the potentials of design science for innovation practice in industry.

5   Results and Observations

The results from the initial round of the Delphi study helped us focus in on several key advantages and disadvantages of design science as the future of innovation practice. In this section, we briefly list these observations and refine our research question as a segue to on-going research, including a second round of the Delphi method.

5.1   Design Science Advantages

An initial observation was that nearly all practitioners agree that current innovation processes do not meet the needs in their organizations for producing new and better products and processes. They believe that new ideas are needed. Innovation practitioners found the following design science concepts have clear potential for improving current innovation practices:

1. Design Science provides a unifying language and set of concepts to discuss innovation. The idea that an innovation must provide an identifiable contribution to knowledge resonated with the practitioners.
2. Design Artifacts (Guideline 1) – They felt this guideline was important to support the clear identification of the deliverables of the innovation process as well-defined **Artifacts.**
3. Design Evaluation (Guideline 3) – Many felt this was missing in current innovation practice. They recognized the need for well-defined measures of 'goodness' that provide **Evidence** for innovation utility.
4. Scientific Rigor and Knowledge Contribution (Guidelines 4/5) – While some had concerns on the overuse of rigor (see below), many practitioners praised the need for appropriate, rigorous use of existing **Knowledge** to ground the construction and evaluation of innovations in their organizations.
5. Stakeholder Communication (Guideline 7) – Practitioners cited the difficulties of communicating innovation processes and artifacts effectively to diverse stakeholders with different goals and needs.

5.2   Design Science Challenges

The practitioners expressed a number of significant concerns on the difficulties of introducing the new and more exacting design science concepts and processes into their organization innovation practices:

1. Practitioner Communication – The presentation of design science in the research literature is too academic. More effective presentation materials that speak to practitioners are needed.
2. Emphasis on Science is a Turn-off – There was consensus that scientific rigor is difficult to sell. We need better techniques for overcoming resistance to more scientific methods.
3. Speed to Market – There was clear concern that design science innovation processes will slow things down. As an example, current innovation practices include little to no time to thoroughly survey existing knowledge.
4. Creative Ideas – The design science methods do not address how good ideas are found. Will improved innovation processes lead to better ideas being generated?
5. Costs of Implementing Design Science Innovation – Costs in time and money to support the new design science methods may be high. Practitioners asked about needs for training and tools to support the more rigorous practices of artifact construction and evaluation.
6. Return on Investment – How is the success of Design Science measured? Why should we implement a new innovation process based on design science if we cannot predict the payoff?

6   Conclusions and Future Directions

The results from our first Delphi study round provide convincing evidence that innovation practitioners recognize the need for improved innovation processes and that design science ideas hold clear potential for such future improvements. These findings align with current discussions in the innovation community that effective innovation projects must 'advance science *and* solve significant problems.' (Dugan and Gabriel 2013) A major concern for any firm relying on its ability to manage and develop innovation is how to bridge (long-term) scientific objectives and (short-term) demands for financial performance and other managerial objectives. Thus, innovation managers must become better equipped for understanding the science-based approach toward innovation and the value propositions for the different innovation stakeholders. (Gregor and Hevner 2014)

For future research directions, we plan to continue to a second Delphi method round with the same set of conference participants. Based on the results of the first round, we are developing a more focused set of questions to be addressed to this group via teleconferences and email discussions. We hope to supplement the Delphi data with additional interviews and focus groups involving innovation leaders (e.g. Chief Innovation Officers and innovation managers) in industry, academia, and government. We are investigating opportunities to apply design science methods in one or more industrial innovation projects as research case studies. The use of mixed research methods will provide multiple views on how design science ideas and processes can be transferred and integrated into innovation practice.

Acknowledgements. We acknowledge the invaluable support of the Marcus-Evans group for help with the planning and logistics of the meetings during the innovation conference. The ideas in this paper were refined and improved via discussions with Brian Donnellan and Shirley Gregor.

References

1. Anderson, J., Donnellan, B., Hevner, A.: Exploring the relationship between design science research and innovation: A case study of innovation at Chevron. In: Helfert, M., Donnellan, B. (eds.) EDSS 2011. CCIS, vol. 286, pp. 116–131. Springer, Heidelberg (2012)
2. Baumol, W.: The Free-Market Innovation Machine: Analysing the Growth Mechanism of Capitalism. Princeton University Press, Princeton (2002)
3. Cross, N.: Design Thinking: Understanding How Designers Think and Work. Berg, Oxford and New York (2011)
4. Dugan, R., Gabriel, K.: "Special Forces" Innovation: How DARPA Attacks Problems. Harvard Business Review 91(10), 74–84 (2013)
5. Gregor, S., Hevner, A.: The Knowledge Innovation Matrix (KIM): A Clarifying Lens for Innovation. Informing Science: The International Journal of an Emerging Transdiscipline 17, 217–239 (2014)
6. Hevner, A., March, S., Park, J., Ram, S.: Design Science in Information Systems Research. Management Information Systems Quarterly 28(1), 75–105 (2004)
7. Hevner, A.R., Donnellan, B., Anderson, J.: The DRIVES (Design research for innovation value, evaluation, and sustainability) model of innovation. In: Helfert, M., Donnellan, B. (eds.) EDSS 2012. CCIS, vol. 388, pp. 144–154. Springer, Heidelberg (2013)
8. Innovaro. Innovation Briefings - Innovation Leaders 2008 (2008), http://www.innovaro.com
9. Kelley, T., Littman, J.: The Art of Innovation: Lessons in Creativity from IDEO, America's Leading Design Firm. Doubleday, New York (2001)
10. Lindstone, H., Turoff, M.: The Delphi Method: Techniques and Applications. Addison-Wesley, Inc., Reading (1975)
11. Simon, H.: The Sciences of the Artificial, 3rd edn. MIT Press, Cambridge (1996)

Two Hurdles to Take for Maximum Impact
of Design Science Research in the IS-Field

Joan van Aken

Design Science Researh institute
vanaken@dsri.eu

Abstract. Design science research (DSR) in the IS-field is getting more and more an accepted place. Yet it has still not yet realized its full potential impact. I suggest in this conceptual article that design science researchers need to take two hurdles to realize maximum impact of their publications. The first one is taken by explaining to editors, reviewers and readers the nature of DSR contributions in general and their fundamental differences with explanatory contributions: the model one uses in DSR for IS is engineering research, rather than physics, for many the mother of all academic research. The iconic contributions of DSR are well analysed and validated generic design models. Design theories are not about explaining nature, but about artefacts, realized on the basis of generic design models, producing desired effects in given contexts. The second hurdle is to be taken by explaining the special nature of design science contributions in the IS-field: information systems are socio-technical systems. Design science for their 'hard' technical components is much like design science for engineering, but design science and design science research for their 'soft' components is different. In actual designing these differences include issues in the evaluation and realization of designs and in design science research the validation and generalization of designs. These differences are discussed as well as strategies to deal with them.

1 Introduction

Design science (DS) and design science research (DSR) are getting more and more an accepted place in IS-research (March and Smith, 1995; Hevner et al., 2004; Gregor and Hevner, 2013). Nevertheless, DSR has yet to realize its full potential impact, due to gaps in the understanding of its nature, application potential and of its methodology (Gregor and Hevner, 2013).

Gregor and Hevner (2013) address this issue by calling for better explanations to editors and reviewers of the special nature of IS design research contributions. They articulate the types of DSR-contributions to the knowledge base of the IS-field, discuss the nature of theory in design research and develop a knowledge contribution framework and a format for presenting DSR-contributions in academic journals. The present conceptual article follows their call for better explaining IS-design research contributions and builds on their work. It defines two hurdles to take for realizing full understanding and thus full impact of these contributions.

M. Helfert et al. (Eds.): EDSS 2013, CCIS 447, pp. 28–40, 2014.

The first hurdle is to explain the nature of DSR-contributions in general by defining DSR-contributions squarely on the basis of the design paradigm. Many researchers feel that the model to follow in *any* academic research is the explanatory model of physics and that physics research provides norms for *all* kinds of academic research. However, there are fundamental differences between the explanatory paradigm of e.g. physics and sociology and the design paradigm of e.g. engineering and medicine (van Aken, 2004 and 2005). These differences are not always fully understood by non-designers and this has consequences for the definition and assessment of DSR-contributions. Taking the first hurdle for full understanding is to be taken by explaining that the model followed by IS-design science research is engineering research rather than physics.

But there is also a second hurdle of misunderstandings to take. This one is caused by the special nature of information systems, the consequences of which are not always fully recognized. Information systems are socio-technical systems, i.e. complex arrangements of hardware, software, procedures, data and people (March and Smith, 1995). Design in information systems is not only about the design of technical artefacts. It is also about designing and changing social practice to realize desired effects in which the technical artefact plays a pivotal role (Sjöström, 2010). As will be discussed, the behaviour of technical (or material) systems is governed by 'strong mechanisms', while the behaviour of social systems is governed by 'weak mechanisms' (van Aken, 2013). Because of this, material systems are often called 'hard' systems and social systems 'soft' ones. One may conceptualize an information system as a 'hard' system of hard and software components[1], embedded in a 'soft' social system of users, user processes, and user capabilities and attitudes. This makes that design science as well as design science research for IS-systems differs from engineering design. Hard systems are expected to behave as designed, so also non-designers can understand that design knowledge on hard systems can be valid and valuable. However, human agency makes that 'soft' social systems do not necessarily behave as designed. Designs can influence human behaviour, but do not determine it. If this is true, what, then, are the nature, validity and value of design knowledge for 'soft' systems[2]? So the second hurdle is to explain these differences and the approaches and methodologies needed in DSR for socio-technical systems.

The article starts with giving definitions of DS and DSR. Also a distinction will be made within design science research between design questions and knowledge questions.

Next the first hurdle, misunderstanding the nature of design research contributions, is discussed on the basis of the model of engineering design. First by giving a brief analysis of designing in engineering, followed by a discussion of engineering design research. Well analysed and validated *generic design models* can be regarded as the iconic DSR-contributions, in engineering research as well as in IS-research.

---

[1] From the perspective of IT-hardware software may look soft (nomen est omen), but from the perspective of social system design the combination of hard and software is 'hard' enough to allows almost fully the approaches and methodologies of 'hard' engineering design.

[2] Soft systems is a concept coined by Checkland (see e.g. Checkland and Scholes, 1990), but this article does not use his various concepts and methodology, however important they are.

However, this is a necessary but not sufficient explanation and justification of DSR-contributions in IS-research. This is because human agency introduces an element of non-determinism in IS-design which makes generalization of design models difficult. This issue produces the second hurdle. To prepare the discussion on this second hurdle the article proceeds with a brief discussion on social system design and its differences with material system design. These differences include issues in the evaluation of designs, the realization of designs and of the role of the so-called 'hidden properties'. The generalization issue is discussed in the following section on DSR for social system design. This involves a discussion on the differences between the strong mechanisms of the material world and the weak mechanisms of the social world, governing human behaviour. Then the second hurdle is addressed by arguing that well analysed and validated generic design models can also be regarded as iconic DSR-contributions in the IS-field. However, the way in which these design models are to be used in designing in the field and the way in which valid and valuable generic design models are developed and validated differ from engineering design. Rigour in developing design knowledge for social systems is quite possible, but is does involve a type of science that differs from physics. The article ends with a discussion and a conclusion.

2   Design Science and Design Science Research

Articles on DS and DSR do not always define what is meant by these two concepts, but in an article intending to define DSR-contributions this seems to be useful. The following definitions are from van Aken (2013), who follows Cross (1993 and 1995). These definitions do not differ from most common sense understandings of these concepts.

'Science' can be defined as a body of knowledge ('scientia' being Latin for knowledge), i.e. valid knowledge produced by rigorous academic research. Design science can be defined as such a body of knowledge on designs and designing to be used in an instrumental way. The addition in this definition on instrumental use draws on the distinction Pelz (1978) makes between instrumental and conceptual use of knowledge. In case of conceptual use knowledge is used for general enlightenment on the subject in question, while instrumental use involves acting on knowledge in specific and direct ways.

Design science research is simply research producing design science. DSR is driven by field problems. A field problem can be defined as a situation in reality, which according to (some or all) stakeholders can or should be improved. In DSR the field problem is translated into a design problem: what (realized) design can solve the field problem or at least improve the problem situation? DSR does not only deal with these design problems, but also with knowledge problems, that is with questions about the behaviour and effects of artefacts (realized designs) in context[3].

---

[3] This distinction between design problems and knowledge problems draws on Wieringa (2009). However, Wieringa does not make a distinction between field problems and design problems, combining these problems by using the term 'practical problems'.

Like any academic research, DSR aims at generic knowledge. A DSR-project is driven by a *type* of design problem, derived from a class of field problems, like the need or desire for improving a certain type of business function or the wish to exploit a new IT-technology in the field.

3   The First Hurdle: The Design Model as the Iconic Design Science Research Contribution

The fundamental differences between research based on the explanatory paradigm and research based on the design paradigm (van Aken, 2004, 2005) are a major source of misunderstandings. Not only for non-designers, but quite often also for designers as they try to meet apparent general criteria for valid knowledge and for rigorous research, which are almost invariably based on the ones for explanatory research. Explanatory research, main stream research in e.g. physics and sociology, is a *search* for understanding, and natural laws or causal mechanisms can be *discovered*. Design, on the other hand, deals with the world that can be. One cannot search for this world, nor can it be discovered, because it does not (yet) exist. The world that can be is to be designed and designing always involves a creative jump to something new (abduction[4]), be it a small jump in incremental design or a large one in radical design. Abduction plays a key role in dealing with design questions. For knowledge questions the research strategies and methods of explanatory research can be used.

The model followed by DSR in the IS-field (consciously or unconsciously) is not physics, but engineering research, like research in mechanical, civil or electrical engineering. The iconic DSR-contribution in engineering research is the well analysed and validated generic design model, like a design for a new transmission system for cars, or for a new way to build bridges in unstable riverbeds or a new design for electronic receivers at higher frequencies than usual.

Generic design models have a key function in the design process. Designing is done in synthesis-evaluation iterations (Roozenburg and Eekels, 1995). In the synthesis step one makes a version of a design that may solve the design problem and may satisfy the requirements, made for the design. In the evaluation step one analyses ex-ante the design 'on paper' to see whether it meets specifications. If that is (not yet) the case, an adapted design is made and again evaluated. These iterations are continued until a satisfactory design has been made (see also van Aken, van der Bij and Berends, 2012, on this process). Generic design models play an important role in the synthesis step. Designing is typically *variant design*, in which a variant is made of a known generic design model. In incremental design the variant can stay close to the design model, but one can also make a big jump to something very different on certain properties of the design model as in radical design. But even in radical design the exploration for possible radical solutions for the design problem still uses to some

---

[4] See e.g. Pierce (1923) or Samuels (2000) on abduction, and Roozenburg and Eekels (1995) and Van Aken et al. (2012) on the role of abduction in designing. Abduction plays a key role in dealing with design problems, but the earlier mentioned knowledge problems can be dealt with by using the research strategies of explanatory research.

extent generic design models. Furthermore, every engineering discipline uses a specific 'design language' to describe its designs during the design process and to communicate its final designs through e.g. texts and drawings with the people who have to realize them in workshops or construction sites. The layperson, not having mastered this language, is not able to 'read' the designs made in the discipline in question.

For the evaluation step engineers have a lot of engineering mathematics at their disposal to set the values of the various parameters of their designs and to evaluate their designs 'on paper'. Evaluation on paper is the evaluation of a 'paper design' (even if computers are used to do this job) to decide whether or not to transfer this design to physical reality. If the design is too complex to analyse their design mathematically, engineers can use *case-based reasoning*[5], which involves an analysis of their 'paper design' by comparing it with similar well analysed and documented *realized* designs (which is, of course, much more difficult in radical design than in incremental design).

As said, the iconic DSR-product is the generic design model. Typically it is made by realizing and field-testing a series of instantiations until a version is made that satisfies the researchers. This final version is further field-tested to validate it. Validation[6] of a design model is gathering evidence for the core claim of design science research. This core claim with respect to a generic design model is that realized artefacts, made on the basis of this generic design model, will produce the desired and claimed performance. As will be discussed, because of the strong mechanism in the material world engineering design needs in principle only one test to get sufficient evidence for this core claim. Like Galileo also needed but one test to prove that small balls fall equally fast as big ones.

I suggest that also IS-design science research can present its results in terms of well analysed and validated generic design models. Design theories are not about explaining nature, but about artefacts, realized on the basis of generic design models, producing desired effects in given contexts (Wieringa, 2009), preferably with explanations on why, through what mechanisms, the use of the artefact produces the desired effects. Examples of generic design models in IS are a type of Enterprise Resource Planning system, a type of expert system or a type of office automation system. Like discussed under engineering design, such generic design models can be used in variant design to design context-specific instantiations[7]. A type of information system can be used a generic design model if it is well analysed, if it is validated and if it is known through what mechanisms its effects are produced.

---

[5] See e.g. Leake (1996) or Watson (1996) on case-based reasoning for evaluating material system designs.

[6] In this article the *validation* of a generic design model to prove the core claim associated with this generic design model, is distinguished from the *evaluation* of a paper design for a specific application as discussed earlier in the context of the synthesis-evaluation iterations.

[7] Gill and Hevner (2013) use the term 'fitness' for instantiations that can be reproduced (in analogy with biology, where the fitness of a given organism is its ability to reproduce within a given ecosystem). In the terms of this article an instantiation with a proven high 'fitness' can be regarded as a generic design model.

As said, the validation of a generic design model is about the potential of artefacts, realized on the basis of the design model in question, to produce through their use desired effects in given contexts. What effects are to be desired is to be defined by their (future) stakeholders. The validation of a generic design model is not about the definition of desired effects themselves, but about the realization of already established desired effects.

This use of generic design models to design specific instantiations is a mode of generalization. One instantiation is generalized to a series of instantiations with similar properties producing the desired effects. It is not the statistical, sample-based generalization of quantitative social science research in which propositions are generalized from samples to populations *as they are*. It is instead the mode of generalization, called analytic generalization by Yin (1984), in which generic propositions are transferred from the settings in which they have been developed to other contexts, while being *translated and contextualized* on the basis of a careful analysis of the differences between the target context and the (average) source contexts[8].

March and Smith (1995) give the following, well-known, types of DSR-contributions in the IS-field: constructs, models, methods and instantiations. These can be interpreted in terms of generic design models. Constructs can be regarded as elements of the 'design language' of IS-design to be used in describing generic design models as well as individual specific designs. Models and methods are typically already presented as design models (without using this term), being generic proposals for making specific designs of for following a course of action to achieve a given objective. Finally, instantiations provide evidence for the validation of the generic design model, showing that designs made on the basis of the generic design model do indeed produce the desired effects. However, as we will see, unlike in engineering design, one instantiation is seldom enough to validate a design model.

In aiming in research for developing generic design models and subsequently presenting them to editors, reviewers and readers as key DSR-contributions in the IS-field, one should also follow Gregor and Hevner's (2013) call for in-depth explanations. A generic design model is a type of research contribution that differs from the explanatory theories and causal models of most common research, also in IS, and thus needs explaining and justification.

But there is a second hurdle to take because of the special nature of IS-design. Unlike engineering design IS-design does not only operate in the material world but also in the social one. In the social world human agency introduces elements of non-determinism in the behaviour of realized designs and that makes that both the development of design science and the use of design science differs from engineering design. Design models can be the iconic DSR-contribution also in IS-research, but they need a further explanation: the second hurdle. In order to develop this explanation the following section gives a brief discussion on social system design and the following one on social system design research.

---

[8] See Lee and Baskerville (2003) on a thorough discussion of the issue of generalization and the various modes of generalization.

4   Social System Design

Although some believe that social systems cannot be designed, but are emergent, social system design is a routine business process in almost any organization. New company structures or departmental structures or business processes are routinely designed and implemented. Even if implementation of a social system design has its problems, in general social system design can be done with reasonable success. What is true, however, is that social system designs do not determine system behaviour like designs for material systems do and that a significant part of a realized social system is indeed emergent: the so-called informal organization[9]. What is also true is that quite often social system design, and in particular implementation, is done in a non-professional way.

Social system design has many similarities with engineering design. These include

- the use of design requirements (why make a new design and what are the demands for the new system)
- gathering relevant input for the design process (like an analysis of the problem that triggered the design process and its context)
- executing the core design process in synthesis-evaluation iterations
- the use of generic design models for the synthesis step (like the functional, business-unit of geographical organization structure and the very idea of the superior-subordinate structure)
- the ex-ante evaluation of designs 'on paper'
- the documentation of the final design in a way that it can be realized by others.

However, social system design is not always done in a professional way. Because of the above-mentioned similarities, it can learn a lot from engineering design (see van Aken et al., 2012). Typically the elements of the design process mentioned above are done in a very informal way, more visible in an analysis by an observer, than consciously executed by the designers. From engineering design one can for instance learn

- rigorous attention for the design requirements and the need to get full understanding and consensus of the various stakeholders on these
- rigorous attention for the inputs (and their quality) to the design process, like these specifications, the analysis of problem and its context, and relevant generic design knowledge like design models and general industry knowledge
- and in particular attention for the rigorous ex-ante evaluation 'on paper' of the design.

There are also fundamental differences between engineering design and social system design. One is the ex-ante evaluation 'on paper' of designs. In engineering design one can often use mathematical modelling and analysis (or simulation) to evaluate designs on paper, but the indeterminate nature of social systems designs makes this infeasible.

---

[9] See e.g. Gray and Starke (1988) on the informal organization.

Therefore, like has been discussed for certain complex instances in engineering design, also in social system design case-based reasoning can be used as an important method for the evaluation of designs.

The second fundamental difference is in the realization of the design. In material system design the design can be realized by a workshop, factory of construction firm largely as it has been designed. A good design gives them all the information they need to do so. In social system design the design is realized by the members of the (new) system by internalizing the design. This involves a redesign of the formal design: the interpretation and appropriation of the formal design from the perspective of the actors who have to operate in the new system. This realization of a design has also to deal with the fact that often social system design is a 'brown field' and not a 'green field' design and thus involves a redesign of an existing situation. Therefore this interpretation and appropriation step has been called 'the second redesign'. This second redesign and the subsequent phase of 'learning to perform' in the new situation (involving further adaptations of the formal design), leads to the emergence of the informal organization (see van Aken, 2007, on this process of second redesign, realization and emergence).

The emergent informal organization can be discussed in terms of 'hidden properties'. Any *realized* design – material and social alike – has unlimited hidden properties, properties present in reality but not in the design that was used to realize it. For instance, the colour of the housing of a machine may be a hidden property: the designer did not specify it in the design because he/she felt that this property is unimportant and left it to the workshop to choose the colour. Good designers only specify in their designs the properties that are important for the performance of the realized design.

In social system design one can regard the informal organization as the hidden properties of the realized social system, not specified in the formal design, but present in social reality. But, contrary to material system design, the hidden properties of a realized social system typically have an important impact on performance. Therefore, designers or change agents have to monitor the second redesign and the learning to perform and to intervene if deemed necessary for performance (see van Aken, 2007, on hidden properties and the importance of the informal organization).

5   Social System Design Research

I have suggested that the iconic product of design science research is the well analysed and validated generic design model, both for material system and for social system design research. The core scientific claim associated with a generic design model is that its application (in the given application domain) will indeed produce the desired effects: the validation issue. So the core issue in DSR (again both in the material and social world) is the prediction of system performance. The golden standard for this is field testing, the testing of instantiations of the design in various contexts within its intended application domain.

In the material world this prediction of system performance through field testing does not pose specific methodological problems, different from methodological issues in developing valid explanations. The reason for this is that in the material world there are *invariant, universal, individual behaviour determining mechanisms.* An electron does not have the freedom to act tomorrow differently from today, nor in New York differently from Amsterdam. A machine, developed, assembled and tested in Helsinki, will work next month likewise in Dublin. Through these mechanisms in the material world the test results on one instantiation of a given research product (for which standard analytical methodologies of explanatory research can be used) can be readily generalized to other times and places. '

This applies to engineers and to some lesser extent also to medical doctors[10]. However, in the social world there are no universal, invariant, individual behaviour determining mechanisms. Therefore, the prediction of system performance in the social world is difficult. In the social world the evaluation of one application of a generic design model cannot simply be generalized to other times and places. This is the fundamental methodological problem of design science research in the social world. It is caused by human agency.

Even if there are no behaviour determining mechanisms in the social world, there are regularities and patterns in social behaviour. In fact, the prediction (within certain ranges) of the behaviour of other people in response to one's own behaviour is an almost universal human competence. Without this competence intentional social behaviour would be impossible. The extent to which this competence is important and universal can be seen in people, lacking this competence because of an autistic disorder.

This competence is developed by personal social experiential learning, learning from personal social experiences[11]. It is subsequently applied through case-based reasoning: the present setting is compared – typically unconsciously – with similar prior experiences and a line of action is chosen on the basis of the effects of the actions in these previous experiences. This makes that this mode of personal learning is limited by the scope of one's personal experiences: outside this scope the competence of predicting human behaviour is much less, as can be seen when acting in a very different culture than one's own.

Personal experiential social learning is the basis for the social behaviour of any person. However, experiential social learning can also be done in a scientific way: *systematic and objective experiential social learning.* By 'objective' I mean that the strategy includes the use of methods to eliminate as good as possible personal biases in the articulation of the results of experiential learning (like is done in rigorous case-studies). Through this research strategy one can learn what the effects of certain types of interventions in various social settings can be.

Research as systematic and objective experiential social learning is learning on the basis of series of rigorous case-studies with detailed descriptions and analyses of problem, context, interventions and effects, giving deep insight in these elements and in their interrelations. This approach has been called 'Action Design Research' by Sein et al. (2011) or 'Technical Action Research' by Wieringa and Morali (2012).'Thick' descriptions, as opposed to the strongly reductionistic models of quantitative research, are needed to make the reading of case-studies into 'real' social

---

[10] This 'lesser extent' is due to the fact that in testing interventions medical doctors deal with living material of which there are never exact copies in other times and places, so they need RCT's or other sophisticated research designs to generalize test results.

[11] See e.g. Kolb (1984) on the power of experiential learning.

experiences. So the experiential learning strategy involves series of rigorous case-studies on a certain type artefact in various contexts within the intended application domain. These case-studies can be executed in 'Action Research mode', in which case the researcher is involved in developing and testing the intervention, but the researcher can also take a more observer role, observing how others develop and use interventions to address the field problem.

The research is to be made 'objective' by using the various methods of rigorous case-studies, like controlled observations, triangulation, 'thick' descriptions, careful cross-case analyses and member checks and by alfa- and beta-testing of the developed interventions or systems.

Scientific experiential learning through series of case-studies involves working alternating in the *practice stream* and in the *knowledge stream* (Andriessen, 2007). In the practice stream one operates in the swamp of practice on a specific instantiation of the generic artefact to be studied, interacting with the various local stakeholders. In the knowledge stream one operates on the high ground of generic theory to generalize the findings of the various individual case-studies through careful cross-case analyses. While interacting with other researchers and with practitioners interested in developing generic theory, one tries to establish what is case-specific on the one hand and what can be learnt from these cases for use in other settings on the other.

Like in personal experiential learning the application of what has been learnt is done through case-based reasoning. System performance is predicted on the basis of a qualitative comparison with interventions in similar settings, somewhat like judges using case-law in determining verdicts.

Experiential social learning is for the researcher the basis strategy to develop generic design models. It is also the basis for the application of generic design models in the field. On the basis of rich case material (the basis of social learning) the practitioner *learns* to understand the system to be redesigned and how variations in context can influence performance.

6 The Second Hurdle; the Nature and Development of IS-Design Science Research Contributions

The thesis of this article is that the iconic product of DSR in the IS-field can be a well-analysed and validated generic design model, just like in engineering research. To explain this well to editors, reviewers and readers is the first hurdle to take for realizing maximum impact.

The second hurdle to take is to deal with understandable objections, based on the differences between engineering research and IS-research. Or, in other words, the differences between material system and social system design and design research. As discussed, these differences are caused by human agency and by the differences between strong material mechanisms and weak social ones. Above the ways to deal with this in social system design and in social system research have been discussed. The main element of taking the second hurdle may be the acceptance that the social world needs another type of science than the material world and that systematic and objective experiential social learning can be the rigorous way to develop generic design models for the social world.

7   Discussion

This article is about design science research. Non design science researchers may call it prescriptive or normative research. This is, however, a misnomer. Researchers cannot and should not from the high ground of theory tell people in the swamp of practice (to use the terms of Schön, 1983) what to do. DSR-publications seldom use the words 'should' of 'ought'. The key product of DSR, the generic design model, is not a normative statement nor a prescription but only a well analysed and validated option, presented to practitioners to be used in their variant designing.

The strategy of systematic and objective experiential social learning may look unfamiliar to researchers with a sound training in research methodology, not in the least because it is not (yet) discussed in methodology textbooks. However, this possible unfamiliarity only exists at the level of research strategy with its design orientation (hurdle one) and its strategy of systematic and objective experiential social learning (hurdle two). It does not exist at the level of execution: in principle in DSR one can confine one's methods for data gathering and analysis to well proven ones. Furthermore, for the well-trained researcher the strategy may look unfamiliar, but it is a very naturalistic approach. It is what everybody does who wants to realize desired effects by a new intervention in a possibly new context: he or she applies the intervention a few times and learns by doing how to realize these desired effects. Finally, for DSR in the IS-field the strategy may even look fairly familiar, because of the publications on e.g. Action Design Research (Sein et al., 2011) and Technical Action Research (Wieringa and Morali, 2012). Using the term 'systematic and objective experiential social learning' is, however, not a semantic issue. This term is used because of its emphasis on rich descriptions to allow social learning and because of the nature of the intended products of this research strategy: not formulae or instructions, but deep insight in the complexities of the relations between information systems and effects and of the various contextual influences on these effects.

My background is in management research and design science research. My interest in IS-research is to a large extent driven by the combination in IS-design and research of hard material systems and soft social ones. This makes it possible to research and show the power of material system design, in particular in engineering design, and the fundamental differences between material and social system design.

Finally I would like to suggest that the idea of the double hurdle is not only applicable in DSR in the IS-field, but also in DSR in most social sciences: the first hurdle of understanding the differences between classical explanatory research (like in physics) and intervention, or improvement or design oriented research (like in engineering and medicine) is present in most social sciences. But the second hurdle is also present in most social sciences. This is the hurdle of understanding that intervention or design oriented research in the social world demands a kind of science, differing from the kind of science possible in the material world. This demand is caused by human agency and by the differences between the strong mechanisms of the material world and the weak mechanisms of the social world.

8   Conclusion

Behaviour in the intangible, fluid and indeterminate social world of human agency and human relations is not governed by the strong mechanisms of the material world, but by the weak mechanisms of the social one. As said, this necessitates a different type of science. Instead of measuring, mathematical modelling and application of mathematical (causal) models through logical deduction, one has systematic and objective experiential social learning.

For editors, reviewers and readers DSR in the IS-field is getting more and more an accepted place, but it's fundamental differences with explanatory research are still too little understood (the first hurdle to take), as well as the differences between the design of material systems (engineering design) and social system design, and the associated need for a different type of science[12], the second hurdle to take. So, in order to realize full impact of DSR in IS, it is important to follow the call of Gregor and Hevner (2013) by explaining in full detail the above-mentioned differences.

References

1. Andriessen, D.: Designing and testing an OD-action, Reporting Intellectual Capital to Develop Organizations. Journal of Applied Behavioural Science 43(1), 89–107 (2007)
2. Checkland, P., Scholes, J.: Soft Systems Methodology in Action. Wiley, Chichester (1990)
3. Cross, N.: 'Science and Design Methodology: a Review'. Research in Engineering Design 5, 63–69 (1993)
4. Cross, N.: Editorial. Design Studies 16, 2–3 (1995)
5. Gill, T.G., Hevner, A.R.: A Fitness Utility Model for Design Science Research. ACM Transactions on Management Information Systems 4(2), article 5 (2013)
6. Gray, J.L., Starke, F.A.: Organization Behavior: Concepts and Applications, 4th edn. Merrill Publishing Company, Columbus (1988)
7. Gregor, S.: The Nature of Theory in Information Systems. MIS-Quarterly 30(3), 611–642 (2006)
8. Gregor, S., Hevner, A.R.: Positioning and Presenting Design Science Research for Maximum Impact. MIS-Quarterly 37(2), 337–355 (2013)
9. Hevner, A.R., March, S.T., Park, J., Ram, S.: Design Science in Information Systems Research. MIS Quarterly 28(1), 75–105 (2004)
10. Kolb, D.A.: Experiential learning: Experience as the source of learning and development. Prentice-Hall, Englewood Cliffs (1984)
11. Leake, D.B.: Case-Based Reasoning: Experiences, Lessons and Future Directions. American Association for Artificial Intelligence, Menlo Park (1996)
12. Lee, A.S., Baskerville, R.L.: Generalizing Generalizability in Information Systems Research. Information System Research 14(3), 221–243 (2003)
13. March, S.T., Smith, G.F.: Design and natural science research in information technology. Decision Support Systems 15, 251–266 (1995)

---

[12] At least for prospective design science research, where human behavior is non-determined. In retrospective explanatory research there is no longer an impact of human agency: one can treat past human action as fixed.

14. Pelz, D.S.: Some expanded perspectives on the use of social science in public policy. In: Yinger, M., Cutler, S.J. (eds.) Major Social Issues: A Multidisciplinary View, pp. 346–357. Free Press, New York (1978)
15. Pierce, C.S.: Chance, Love and Logic: Philosophical Essays. Kegan Paul, London (1923)
16. Roozenburg, N.F.M., Eekels, J.: Product design, Fundamentals and Methods. Wiley, Chichester (1995)
17. Samuels, W.J.: Signs, pragmatism and abduction: the tragedy, irony and promise of Charles Sanders Pierce. Journal of Economic Issues 34(1), 207–217 (2000)
18. Schön, D.A.: The reflective Practitioner. Temple Smith, London (1983)
19. Sein, M.K., Henfridsson, O., Purao, S., Rossi, M., Lindgren, R.: Action Design Research. MIS-Quarterly 35(1), 37–56 (2011)
20. Sjöström, J.: The design of Information Systems, a pragmatic account. Doctoral dissertation, university of Uppsala (2010)
21. Van Aken, J.E.: Management Research on the Basis of the Design Paradigm: the Quest for Field-tested and Grounded Technological Rules. Journal of Management Studies 41(2), 219–246 (2004)
22. Van Aken, J.E.: 'Management Research as a Design Science: articulating the research products of mode 2 knowledge production'. British Journal of Management 16, 19–36 (2005)
23. Van Aken, J.E.: Design Science and Organization Development Actions: Aligning Business and Humanistic Values. Journal of Applied Behavior Science 43(1), 1–17 (2007)
24. van Aken, J.E.: Design science: Valid knowledge for socio-technical system design. In: Helfert, M., Donnellan, B. (eds.) EDSS 2012. CCIS, vol. 388, pp. 1–13. Springer, Heidelberg (2013)
25. Van Aken, J.E., Berends, J.J., Van der Bij, J.D.: Problem Solving in Organizations: A Methodological Handbook for Business Students, 2nd edn. Cambridge University Press, Cambridge (2012)
26. Watson, I.: Applying Case-Based Reasoning: Techniques for Enterprise Systems. Morgan Kaufman Pubs, San Francisco (1998)
27. Wieringa, R.J.: 'Design Science as Nested problem solving'. In: Proceedings of the 4th International Conference on Design Science in Information Systems and Technology, pp. 1–12. ACM, New York (2009)
28. Wieringa, R., Moralı, A.: Technical action research as a validation method in information systems design science. In: Peffers, K., Rothenberger, M., Kuechler, B. (eds.) DESRIST 2012. LNCS, vol. 7286, pp. 220–238. Springer, Heidelberg (2012)
29. Yin, R.: Case-study Research: Design and Methods. Sage, Beverly Hills (1984)

Privacy and Accountability in Online Communities: Towards a Theory of Scrutiny

Jonas Sjöström[1], Pär J. Ågerfalk[1], and Alan R. Hevner[2]

[1] Uppsala University, Sweden
{jonas.sjostrom,par.agerfalk}@im.uu.se
[2] University of South Florida, USA
ahevner@usf.edu

Abstract. Information systems design must balance requirements of privacy and accountability for the good of individuals and society. We ground our study in the context of the design and development of a eHealth system for psychosocial care. Multi-level privacy protections are balanced with the need to provide for accountable interventions in well-defined critical care situations. We identify a set of meta-requirements leading towards a theory of scrutiny.

Keywords: Privacy, Accountability, Online psychosocial care, Anonymity, Design theory.

"No one shall be subjected to arbitrary interference with his privacy, family, home or correspondence, nor to attacks upon his honour and reputation." United Nations: The Universal Declaration of Human Rights [19, article 12]

"Information accountability means the use of information should be transparent so it is possible to determine whether a particular use is appropriate under a given set of rules and that the system enables individuals and institutions to be held accountable for misuse." Weitzner et al. [22].

1 Introduction

The rise of online communities and social media as a vehicle for large-scale social interaction has accelerated the penetration of information technology (IT) into both private and professional life [1]. Arguably, a significant part of contemporary social interaction is mediated by, or planned using, IT. While this evolution of human collaboration and social life may be beneficial in many ways, it also suggests a significant threat to individual privacy. The threat to privacy is fueled by two forces [11]. The first force is the growth of IT, which in itself enables increased surveillance, storage, *et cetera*. The second force is that commercial actors find value in information about individuals, causing them to seek ways to exploit technological opportunities to collect and capitalize on such information. One's right to privacy, i.e. to "freedom from unauthorized intrusion" [14], is a human right as declared by the United Nations as seen in the above quote. The recent turmoil caused by former NSA employee

M. Helfert et al. (Eds.): EDSS 2013, CCIS 447, pp. 41–51, 2014.

Edward Snowden's leaked details of top-secret government mass surveillance programs shows the timeliness and importance of the online privacy discourse.

One way to facilitate privacy is by means of providing anonymity. The topic of *anonymous* interaction between peers in an online community is at the heart of community design. People tend to behave differently in cyberspace than in real life, e.g. say and do things that they would not say or do face-to-face. This shift in behavior is known as the online disinhibition effect [16]. On the one hand, behavior may change in a way that is desired by the community provider, e.g. encouraging people to read and contribute to discussion fora. On the other hand, anonymity creates a risk of undesired behavior that negatively impacts the community provider's intentions, such as bullying or provision of links to buy illegal drugs. There are well-known examples of the consequences of unethical online behavior from discussion fora and online newspapers, such as the closedown of user comments on the Engadget forum [23]. Consequentially, the community provider may need to proactively monitor peer activity, identify undesired behavior, and take action when such behavior occurs. From the community provider perspective, such actions concern accountability, i.e. the means by which to hold people accountable when peer behavior deviates from the norms of the community.

Information accountability relies on transparency in IS design and use [22]. The tension between these two ideals – privacy and accountability – causes a challenge for designers to preserving privacy, while at the same time ensuring accountability. The context of the study at hand – online psychosocial care – puts this tension at the fore. Professional codes of conduct as well as legislation in many countries dictate that whenever a licensed therapist detects potentially suicidal or self-destructive behavior, the therapist has a legal and ethical right to intervene. It must thus be possible to sacrifice anonymity in order to reach the patient even though they are normally anonymous during treatment. From a design point of view, this means that although most caregiving activities are performed with preserved patient anonymity, there is a need to support breach of anonymity in certain well-defined circumstances. It is also critical that information to provide accountability in relation to caregiving actions be logged and maintained even while these actions are anonymous. For example, if a patient files a complaint against a therapist, data must be available to either support or refute the allegation.

To address the challenge, we propose a nascent *theory of scrutiny* – that is, a theory concerned with online interactive environments where privacy is guaranteed while accountability can be maintained and easily inspected. We conceptualize a supportive environment to maintain anonymity, yet preserve a meta-level of accountability and control. Design implications and the generalizability of the proposed concepts are discussed.

2   The U-CARE Project

The system under study was designed and developed as part of a large multi-disciplinary research program, U-CARE. A major component of the project was the implementation of a complex software system for eHealth research, specifically online psychosocial care. The overarching project involves researchers and practitioners from psychology, medicine, information systems, caring sciences, and economics.

The research program aims at supporting people with potentially lethal somatic diseases to cope with posttraumatic stress caused by their diagnosis, which may lead to depression and anxiety. Such stress may also have a negative impact on the treatment of the somatic disease. For example, a depressive state may cause a patient to engage in less physical activity, develop sleeping problems, or forget to adhere to their medications. Internet-based self help has proven effective for psychiatric disorders as well as for promotion of healthy behavior [2, 15]. It is promising both with regard to treatment efficacy and cost, by using less therapist time per effectively treated patient compared to face-to-face therapy [18].

The intended online support is based on a stepped-care strategy, which means that patients with mild depression or anxiety are directed to a self-help program, while patients with more severe depression or anxiety are offered a treatment program based on cognitive behavioral therapy (CBT) [15]. On top of this, patients become part of an online community, allowing them to interact with peers in discussion forums, online chats, and through internal messages.

The design of the online information system required a number of innovation solutions that provided the opportunity for design science research [9, 11] with clear eHealth research relevance. Collaboration with senior researchers as well as practitioners in various fields has improved our understanding of the problem domain and the clinical needs. Different academic traditions (e.g. caring sciences vs. economics) approach eHealth from different angles. The various ideals from each tradition emphasize different aspects of relevance and rigor, since there is a continual need within the group to scrutinize the rationales for design decisions.

Our system design process was set up in accordance with agile values [4], characterized by sprint reviews approximately every two weeks. The review meetings had several recurring members representing different professions and academic disciplines. In addition, external specialists and patient groups were invited to explore the software, followed by workshops in which they provided feedback to the design team. In total, 70+ design workshops were organized, engaging a great variety of stakeholders. IS researchers contributed with knowledge from the IS field and related disciplines (primarily interaction design and software engineering).

A retrospective analysis of the design process reveals five major design cycles related to the development of features to support peer interaction. The design cycles took place from November 2011 to June 2013. Various stakeholders used the emerging software during this period, both in dedicated beta testing activities but also in 'production mode' to upload content, prepare future randomized controlled trials, et cetera. Since May 2012, the software has been used in two pilot studies using real patients for subjects. The early design cycles focused on vanilla functionality for forum, chat, and internal messaging features, while later cycles were oriented towards abuse, privacy, moderation, and accountability issues. We identified the design challenge of balancing privacy requirements with accountability requirements to be a critically important area that has received little rigorous attention in the IS field.

3   Background

Even though privacy is a well-known concept, it has never been as much in focus as it is currently. In addition to the technological development, developments in both the commercial and the public sector have given rise to increasing privacy concerns [16]. Commercial organizations have identified new means to analyze consumers, and government intelligence exploits techniques to identify threats to society by analyzing online activity. Albeit deceptively straightforward, the term 'privacy' is not easily defined. A value-based definition views "general privacy as a human right integral to society's moral value system" [16, pp. 992–993]. While such a definition is highly normative, researchers in Information Systems and other social sciences frequently adopt other views, such as privacy as "the ability of individuals to control the terms under which their personal information is acquired and used" [5, p. 326]. In this work, we subscribe to the normative definition, while still acknowledging that the ability of individuals to maintain control of their information is an important consideration in IS design. A comprehensive survey and meta-analysis of IS research on privacy can be found in Belanger and Crossler [3].

According to ethno-methodologist Harold Garfinkel [6], actions that are accountable are 'visibly-rational-and-reportable-for-all-practical-purposes', a notion that is at the heart also of information accountability in the context of online psychosocial care. In keeping with Weber's [21] classical definition of social action, i.e. that human behaviour to which the actor attaches meaning and which takes into account the behaviour of others and thus is directed in its course, Garfinkel's view suggests that an accountable IS must keep a record of the social actions performed through and by means of the system (both their social grounds and their social purposes) as a sociopragmatic instrument for communication [7].

Weitzner et al. [22] approach accountability from a web infrastructure perspective. They propose three architectural features to be incorporated in the future web to facilitate transparency and information accountability. *First*, policy-aware transaction logs that record "information-use events". Such logs should be kept by each endpoint in a de-centralized system. The point of the logs is that they facilitate follow-up on information use and misuse. *Second*, they point out the need for a common framework to represent policy rules. Semantic web technology would be the foundation for such frameworks, which would emerge through the collaboration of large overlapping communities on the web. *Third*, policy-reasoning tools would support users in understanding how the data they knowingly or unknowingly share may be used. Such information would be made possible through the policy rule frameworks. Our work focuses on the community level (which could be one endpoint in such an infrastructure) at which the architectural features are not directly applicable. The accountability principles behind the architectural features may nonetheless be re-phrased as meta-requirements for accountability in the current context (see Table 1).

Table 1. Meta-requirements drawn from the literature

#	Meta-requirement
MR-1	Transaction logs should be kept in order to facilitate retrospective analysis of important actions in the community.
MR-2	Policies should be defined that clearly state how information that is produced within the community will be used.
MR-3	Policies must be effectively communicated to community peers to support peers in maintaining control over their privacy.

4   The U-CARE Case Study

In this section, we outline the case study, focusing on the design of the software system content specifically in relation to information accountability, privacy, and anonymity. It should be noted that "content" here refers to four different types of user-created content: Forum threads and forum posts, public and private chat messages, internal messages (between peers), and public diary entries. Each type of content is subject to scrutiny, since others may view it. All users – staff as well as patients – are informed about the extensive logging of actions that takes place in the system, as well as the 'netiquette', i.e. the rules of conduct in the community.

From the perspective of individuals, privacy needs to be protected. Sensitive data must not fall into the wrong hands. Data should only be used for treatment, and (if informed consent is given) for other well-specified purposes. Implications for design include a need to adopt state-of-the-art technology and practices to ensure that data are well protected. Authentication and authorization schemes are necessary to appropriately allow access to data. De-identified data and personal identities should kept separate in order to increase security. The privacy issue, however, relates to other stakeholder responsibilities as outlined below.

From a researcher point-of-view, there is a need to keep track of personal identities in order to empower analysis from third party providers (e.g. registry data). A design implication is the adoption of the traditional strategy to store personal identities in a separate place. De-anonymization is facilitated through the application of 'code keys' that enables relating anonymous data to actual individuals. Furthermore, researchers are interested in how the participants act to "consume" psychosocial support online. A design implication is the need to maintain a detailed log of user actions to enable retrospective analyses of use patterns. This log is not limited to patient actions, since the interplay between staff and patients is part of the research interest.

From the caregiver perspective, health staff (e.g. therapists) needs to be able to provide care, insofar as possible without accessing the personal identity of the patients. However, when there is a risk for suicide or self-destructive behavior, there may be a need to 'breech' anonymity to take appropriate action to get in touch with the patient. For design, this means that most caregiving activities are performed with preserved anonymity for the patients. However, there is a need to be able to breech anonymity under certain circumstances.

As healthcare managers and decision makers, there is a need to explore the benefits of new technology, while at the same time maintaining the interests of individuals and professionals. An implication for design is that we need to facilitate follow-ups of privacy breeches to promote accountability. This motivates a logging of actions in general (not only patients) and breeches in particular.

While peer activity in a community is hard to predict, and may peak during non-office hours, there is a need for a filtered content access that supports staff in interpreting activity since the previous scan. Figure 1 shows the community monitor, i.e. the user interface for content scanning.

The bar chart at the top indicates the total amount of interactions per day. Below is a form to filter activity based on various parameters: Sender, recipient, keyword, message type, *et cetera*. A rudimentary abuse function based on keyword scanning provides additional support to staff. Any message that contains an abuse keyword is highlighted. Severe keywords – such as "suicide" – are more emphasized than the message in the example, based on a classification of keyword severity. In addition to the monitoring performed by staff, community peers are in control of their own communication. They may report forum posts, block other users, and personalize how they wish to display their profiles. They may also set their visibility to 'visible' or 'hidden'. In the latter case, no other users can see that they are online.

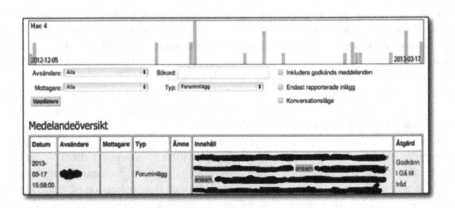

Fig. 1. Screenshot from community monitor view

In order to support staff, a 'moderator manual' was developed by psychologists, researchers, and health staff. The manual describes problems (anomalies) that may occur that require staff intervention. For each problem, there is a suggestion how to address the situation. Table 2 shows an excerpt from the moderator manual. In total, it consists of 15 anomalies, including pornographic content, insults, hate speech, advertising, propaganda *et cetera*. These anomalies represent four categories: Rule violations, medical/therapeutic claims without or contradictory to evidence, negative spirals, and destructive tendencies.

The list of anomalies is there to promote the goals of the organization, in this case to offer an anonymous environment that should promote people's health and healthy behavior. Each anomaly should be understood as a deviation from what is desirable based on a stakeholder responsibility. The anomaly may lead to undesired consequence(s) for stakeholder(s). The negative spirals, for example, may lead to less healthy behavior, which contradicts the organization's goals as a caregiver.

Table 2. Excerpt from the moderator manual

Anomaly	Example	Corrective action(s)
Negative spirals	Patient A states that it is impossible to sleep. Patient B states that s/he tried everything and might as well give up.	Staff intervenes with the aim of breaking the negative spiral using a method with several steps.
Self-destructive or violent tendencies	A discussion evolves around self-destructive or suicidal thoughts.	Immediately contact the responsible therapist(s), who will in turn breech privacy to get in touch with the patient(s). Remove the content.
Respect for others	The real name of another participant is exposed in a public discussion.	Remove the content with a comment why it was removed. Write an internal message to the subject stating that it is not allowed to reveal the identity of other patients.
Promotion of illegal activity	A patient recommends illegal drugs and how to purchase them on the Internet.	Remove the content. Send internal message to the subject informing stating that illegal activities may not be promoted in the community. Contact the police in case there is reason to believe that someone is in danger.

As shown in Table 2, corrective action does not always require the organization to reveal the personal identity of the patient. When identity is revealed, there is a clear rationale for it based on the organization's responsibilities. It is, however, feasible for staff to breech privacy at any given time. Any privacy breech will be logged, and the organization has setup routines to scrutinize breeches. The IT coordinator has the responsibility to extract log data, which are discussed in management meetings each month. Any breech of privacy that is not motivated by anomalies, will be followed-up, which makes it possible to hold staff accountable. Staff members are informed about the privacy rules, both through documents in the organization and in the user interface of the software.

The design of organizational routines as well as software in the U-CARE case aims at compliance with ethical standards and legislation. In the Swedish context, the Swedish Data Inspection Board may audit any organization. In addition, if there are suspicions of misuse of information, the research administrators may follow-up on management of sensitive information.

5   Towards a Theory of Scrutiny

Drawing from our experiences in the design of privacy and accountability in the U-CARE system, we begin the research process of generalizing our findings to a design theory of scrutiny that can be applied to a broader range of IS applications. Here we propose our initial understanding of how best to balance privacy and accountability via an expanded set of meta-requirements [20]. Scrutiny is an activity that involves various stakeholders who engage in different types of action in relation to privacy and accountability. Our design experiences allowed us to differentiate between four 'modes' of scrutiny (Table 3).

Table 3. Four modes of scrutiny

Mode	Scrutinizer	Accountable	Activity
Level 0 Scrutiny	Community member(s)	Community member(s)	Mitigate Community behavior that does not conform to the organizational norms
Level 1 Scrutiny	Staff member(s)	Community member(s)	Mitigate community behavior that does not conform to the organizational norms
Level 2 Scrutiny	Provider Management	Staff member(s)	Log and monitor actions to protect privacy concerns and uphold accountability
Level 3 Scrutiny	External stakeholders	Provider Management	Audit organizations to validate compliance with legislation and ethics.

The conceptual differentiation between these modes provides a structure to analyze an organization with respect to its capabilities to maintain organizational responsibilities and accountability, while protecting individual privacy. We propose that any violation of privacy should be either (i) well-motivated based on organizational responsibility, or (ii) accounted for by someone. Level 3 scrutiny explains the external pressure on organizations to comply with ethics and legislation to uphold privacy and information accountability. This level includes traditional external auditing practices but extends beyond what is legally required to encompass also tacit expectations that external stakeholders may impose on an organization. In order for the organization to respond to such external scrutiny, there is a need for level 2 scrutiny, i.e. internal processes to log and monitor use (and misuse) of sensitive information about individuals. This level is thus comparable to the traditional IT controller function in an organization but goes beyond budgetary control to include employee behavior in a wide sense. Potential misuse may stem from level 1 scrutiny where staff members monitor community activity in a responsible manner in accordance with organizational policies. Privacy concerns are also subject to level 0 scrutiny, which refers to the community members' peer control of, for example, personalization of visibility, their ability to block others, and report content.

The four modes of scrutiny and their interdependencies outline a systematic approach to accountability management in an organization. Any situation where a person is identified during level 1 scrutiny should be justified in keeping with the policies defined in the organization and conform to measures required to maintain level 2 scrutiny, and should be logged for accountability purposes. If a level 3 scrutiny is externally initiated, documentation from level 2 scrutiny serves as an important source to account for the organization's actions.

The design work in the empirical setting continually highlighted trade-offs between accountability and privacy – an example of conflicting desires between the individual and the providing organization. For the organization, there is a need to make balanced and well-informed decisions when to breech privacy [3]. If such decisions are done without appropriate reflection, there is a risk that it will decrease the community's trust in the organization. Unsolicited breech of privacy may also be against ethical standards or legislation. Therefore, in addition to scrutinizing what community peers are doing, there is also a need to scrutinize staff behavior. A systematic approach within the organization to manage level 1 and level 2 scrutiny maintains the provider's capability to respond to level 3 scrutiny, i.e. external parties auditing the provider's compliance with legislation and ethics. Meta-requirements drawn from the literature (Table 1) deal primarily with accountability at levels 0 and 1. Partially, they touch upon level 2 scrutiny since they mention that policies need to be defined that govern accountability issues. However, as shown in Table 4, we add new meta-requirements based on our new theoretical development.

Table 4. Meta-requirements drawn from theoretical development

#	Meta-requirement
MR-4	Follow-ups on content scan and corrective actions should be facilitated to support management in performing level 2 scrutiny.
MR-5	The provider should easily be able to flexibly access documentation that satisfy the requirements from level 3 scrutiny, i.e. external audits of the organization.
MR-6	Staff needs sophisticated support to make sense of ongoing activity in the community. Filtering and analysis need to be supported by technology.
MR-7	Staff actions need to be logged in addition to community member actions. Logging needs to be performed at all times.

Figure 2 shows a set of constructs and relations related primarily to level 1 scrutiny. Scrutinizing the activities in an online community is based on **content scanning**, which requires **content access**. Through scanning, staff may detect an **anomaly** that needs to be mitigated by **corrective action**. Such actions are performed to maintain **stakeholder responsibility**. Examples of corrective actions include blocking a forum post, banning a user from a community, or banning contributions to the discussion. Corrective action may require **actor access**. In some cases, the actor pseudonym is sufficient, e.g. when informing a community member about a rule. In other cases, the true identity of the actor may be required, e.g. when a community member violates legislation. In such cases, it may threaten individual **privacy**. From a provider's point of view, the model suggests that responsibilities should be clarified, and that 'anomalies' in the content that may threaten the organization, need to be mitigated. In the analyzed case study setting, the moderator manual is an example of a design implication of this view.

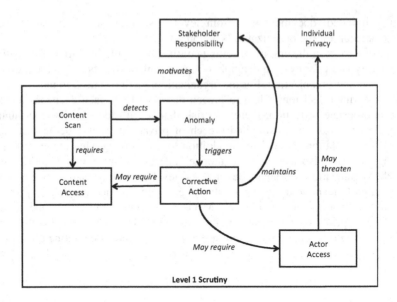

Fig. 2. An emerging model of level 1 scrutiny

6   Discussion

In this paper, we have drawn on our experiences in performing software systems design in the domain of online psychosocial care to develop and propose a 'theory of scrutiny'. The theory addresses the relationships between accountability and privacy, explaining how these concepts relate to the interdependency between four modes of scrutiny. The approach is design based, and addresses the relation between the levels of individual, organization, and society. In doing so, it is a response to the calls for more research on design and action research and multilevel research on privacy [3].

The current version of the theory is a generalization from a single case study [12]. The current empirical setting – online psychosocial care – has served well to explore the problem (due to the sensitive character of personal information). It is, however, easy to find other settings where a community provider needs to relate to both accountability and privacy. Without elaboration, we argue that the theory of scrutiny would make an interesting foundation to inquire into communities of e-learning (e.g. MOOCs), online news, criminology, and scholarly peer review. Community providers in these example settings face similar situations where they provide an environment exposed to and threatened by social and technical vulnerabilities, which resonates with the purpose and scope of the theory.

Although the theoretical contribution at this stage is mainly explanatory [8], we outline the purpose and scope of the theory and a set of tentative meta-requirements. Three were drawn from existing literature (Table 1), four were derived from the theoretical development (Table 4). Future work will include a more detailed analysis of implications for design through a systematic appropriation of meta-theorizing literature in design science research [8, 10, 20].

References

1. Aakhus, M., Ågerfalk, P., Lyytinen, K., Te'eni, D.: Call for Paper: Information Systems for Symbolic Action: Social Media and Beyond. MIS Quarterly (2011)
2. Barak, A., Hen, L., Boniel-Nissim, M., Shapira, N.: A Comprehensive Review and a Meta-Analysis of the Effectiveness of Internet-Based Psychotherapeutic Interventions. Journal of Technology in Human Services 26(2/4), 109–160 (2008)
3. Bélanger, F., Crossler, R.E.: Privacy in the Digital Age: A review of information privacy research in information systems. MIS Quarterly 35(4), 1017–1041 (2011)
4. Conboy, K.: Agility from first principles: Reconstructing the concept of agility in information systems development. Information Systems Research 20(3), 329–354 (2009)
5. Culnan, M.J.: Consumer Privacy, Technology and Policy. In: George, J.F. (ed.) Computers in Society: Privacy, Ethics and the Internet, pp. 171–183. Pearson/Prentice Hall, Upper Saddle River (2003)
6. Garfinkel, H.: Studies in Ethnomethodology. Polity Press, Cambridge (1967)
7. Goldkuhl, G., Agerfalk, P.J.I.: Artefacts as Socio-Pragmatic Instruments: Reconciling the Pragmatic, Semiotic, and Technical. International Journal of Technology and Human Interaction 1(3), 29–43 (2005)
8. Gregor, S.: The Nature of Theory in Information Systems. MIS Quarterly 30(3), 611–642 (2006)
9. Gregor, S., Hevner, A.R.: Positioning and Presenting Design Science Research for Maximum Impact. Mis Quarterly 37(2), 337–355 (2013)
10. Gregor, S., Jones, D.: The anatomy of a design theory. Journal of the Association for Information Systems 8(5), 312–335 (2007)
11. Hevner, A.R., March, S.T., Park, J., Ram, S.: Design science in Information Systems research. Mis Quarterly 28(1), 75–105 (2004)
12. Lee, A., Baskerville, R.: Generalizing Generalizability in Information Systems Research. Information Systems Research 14(3), 221–243 (2003)
13. Mason, R.: Four Ethical Issues of the Information Age. Mis Quarterly 10(1) (1986)
14. Merriam-Webster: Privacy, http://www.merriam-webster.com/dictionary/privacy
15. Riley, S., Veale, D.: The Internet & its Relevance to Cognitive Behavioural Psychotherapists. Behavioural and Cognitive Psychotherapy 27(1), 37–46 (1999)
16. Smith, H.J., Dinev, T.: Information Privacy Research: An interdisciplinary review. MIS Quarterly 35(4), 989–1015 (2011)
17. Suler, J.: The Online Disinhibition Effect. Cyberpsychology and Behavior 7(3), 321–327 (2004)
18. Tate, D., Finkelstein, E.: Cost effectiveness of internet interventions: review and recommendations. Annals of Behavioral Medicine 38(1), 40–45 (2009)
19. United Nations: The Universal Declaration of Human Rights, http://www.un.org/en/documents/udhr/index.shtml
20. Walls, J.G., Widmeyer, G.R., El Sawy, O.A.: Building an Information Systems Design Theory for Vigilant EIS. Information Systems Research 3(1), 36–59 (1992)
21. Weber, M.: Economy and Society. University of California Press, Berkeley (1978)
22. Weitzner, D.J., Abelson, H., Berners-Lee, T., Feigenbaum, J., Hendler, J., Sussman, G.J.: Information accountability. Communications of the ACM 51(6), 82–87 (2008)
23. Zhuo, J.: Where Anonymity Breeds Contempt. The New York Times (2010)

An Approach for Reflectively Discovering and Synthesizing Design Knowledge for Situated Artifacts: The Case of the Early Warning Score Chart

Fred Creedon, John O'Donoghue, Tom O'Kane, Frédéric Adam,
Simon Woodworth, and Siobhán O'Connor

Health Information Systems Research Centre,
University College Cork, O'Rahilly Building, College Road, Cork, Ireland
fredcreedon@gmail.com,
{john.odonoghue,t.okane,
s.woodworth,siobhan.oconnor}@ucc.ie,
fadam@afis.ucc.ie

Abstract. This paper presents an approach for reflectively evaluating systems from a design science perspective. Design science research typically follows a design-build-evaluate methodology, where the evaluation is dependent on the utility requirements defined in the design phase. This methodology is appropriate when designing new systems, but is suboptimal when developing iterative design improvements for existing situated artifacts or legacy systems. For iterative design, there is a necessity to understand the problem system the previous iteration was designed for and what changes to the problem system the artifact was designed to affect. Often the design process for these solutions will not have been adequately documented, and as such a process of discovery must be undertaken to document each stage of the design process. Once documented, an evaluate-build-evaluate design approach can be taken. The purpose of this paper is to outline an approach for acquiring and synthesizing design knowledge, which allows for rigorous evaluation of a situated artifact.

Keywords: Design Science, Design Knowledge, Artifact Evaluation, Situated Artifact, Legacy Systems.

1   Introduction

The result of a design science effort is typically an artifact which when situated in a problem system can affect a required change in a problem system. Normally a *design-build-evaluate* approach is taken when following a design science approach. This is suitable when no existing solution exists, or when previous iterations of the legacy system or artifact have been developed using a design science approach. However, in the case where an iterative design is building an artifact based on an artifact which has not been developed using a design science approach, or little documentation exists regarding the design of the artifact, then a problem exists.

M. Helfert et al. (Eds.): EDSS 2013, CCIS 447, pp. 52–62, 2014.
© Springer International Publishing Switzerland 2014

Design science research has been called *improvement research* [1], and as such before improvements can be made to an existing artifact, it is prudent to develop a thorough understanding of the artifact. Once this understanding has been developed an *evaluate-build-evaluate* approach can be taken.

This paper outlines an approach that can be taken for collecting and synthesizing the design knowledge necessary to rigorously evaluate a situated artifact. This approach identifies the steps in the design science process where knowledge of the problem system, and knowledge of design principles inherent to the class of artifact is synthesized. Suitable methods for discovering and synthesizing this knowledge are identified, and an exemplar in the case of the Irish Health Service Executive's (HSE) EWS Chart is used to demonstrate how the approach can be implemented.

2   An Approach for Synthesizing Design Knowledge for Situated Artifacts

Part of designing an approach for the adequate synthesis of design knowledge for a situated artifact is identifying the design stages knowledge needs to be gathered for. The *process model for procedurally transparent design science research* (PMPT) by Gleasure et al. (2012) was identified as being a suitable model due to it's comprehensive coverage of the stages of the design science process as well as it's emphasis on transparent documentation of the stages. This model was built in an effort to bring together the extant design science model literature, and provide a comprehensive start to finish model that encapsulates each stage of the design science process.

As such only the design stages related to knowledge gathering and hypothesis development were mapped. This approach for *reflective design knowledge synthesis* (RDKS) seeks to establish the knowledge relating to the *utility requirements, kernel knowledge, explanatory/predictive model, and design principles,* which explain the problem system an artifact was developed for, and the design principles instantiated in the artifact which cause the required change in the problem system. While this approach uses these stages from the PMPT model, the sequence in which the knowledge is discovered and synthesized using the RDKS approach differs from the PMPT sequence. This reflects the logical differences between the *design-build-evaluate* approach and the *evaluate-build-evaluate* approach. The following section outlines the steps in the RDKS approach.

3   Steps in the Reflective Design Knowledge Synthesis Approach

The chief contribution of this paper is the RDKS approach, with this section describing each stage of the approach, and the rationale for the sequencing of each of the stages. The approach is presented in *fig. 1*. The motivation for developing this model as described in the previous section was to identify the design knowledge used to develop a situated artifact or legacy system, and synthesize the knowledge in a way that is conducent to empirically evaluating the artifact. Furthermore, the design knowledge synthesized using this approach will be beneficial to the development of further iterations of the artifact.

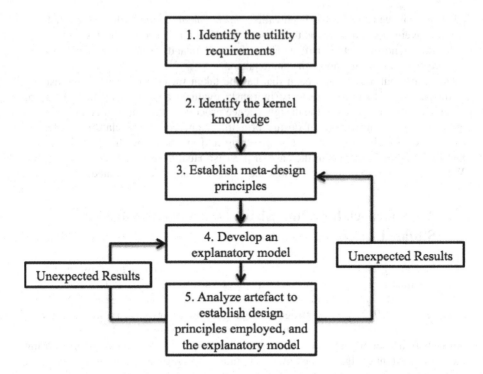

Fig. 1. Process model for the reflective design knowledge synthesis approach

1. Identify the Utility Requirements for the Problem System

The utility requirements refers to the *purpose and scope* of the artifact being evaluated [3]. The artifact being evaluated was developed in order to affect a required change in a problem system [2]. As such it is necessary to understand the problem system, and the changes the artifact is expected to have on the system. In order to establish these utility requirements, exploratory qualitative data collection can be performed. A systematic literature review is an appropriate method for establishing the utility requirements for the artifact being investigated. This review can include industrial or academic literature pertaining to the artifact being investigated. If the utility requirements cannot be abstracted from literature, then it may be necessary to perform interviews or focus groups with individuals involved with the design of the artifact. The result of this step should be a statement or statements describing the problem system and required change the artifact is intended to have on the system.

2. Identify the Kernel Knowledge for the Problem System

Kernel knowledge as utilized by Gleasure (2012)[2] is described as a more detailed description of the problem system identified in step 1. Walls (1992)[4], describes kernel theory as *theories from the natural or social sciences governing the design process itself.* While the PMPT model required the identification of utility requirements prior to this step, there is an understanding that any knowledge synthesized from the identification of kernel knowledge will in turn inform the utility requirements. Having identified the utility requirements for the system, it is then necessary to identify the extant knowledge, and the theories that can explain the problem system. As such it is necessary to search for literature regarding the problem system and study the reference material to establish the extant knowledge, data, and theories that may explain the problem system. If the artifact has been designed employing a design science approach then the kernel knowledge explaining the problem system may already be documented. However, if the available literature regarding the design of the system does not include the kernel knowledge pertaining to the problem system, then there is a necessity to explore and synthesize the kernel knowledge. A systematic literature review is an appropriate method for establishing an adequate coverage of kernel knowledge relating to the problem system. Furthermore, synthesis of this literature can then provide insights into the fundamental theories that explain the problem system.

3. Establish Meta-design Principles

Design-principals as identified in the PMPT model relate to *principles governing the development or selection of system features* [5]. Typically unless an artifact has been designed using a design science approach, the design principles for the artifact will not be documented. However design principles are inherent to any artifact that is designed to make required changes in a problem system. In order to establish the design principles instantiated within the artifact being evaluated, it is useful to identify all possible design principles that are instantiated within the class of artifact being evaluated. A class of artifact relates to a similar set artifacts that are developed to make similar changes in their problem system. In order to identify the meta-design principles, a systematic literature review is appropriate for adequately covering the literature, furthermore this also supports synthesis of the knowledge. By establishing these meta-design principles, a rigorous analysis of the artifact being evaluated is then possible, ensuring that all design-principles instantiated in the artifact being investigated are identified.

4. Develop an Explanatory Model

An explanatory model provides a visual demonstration of the design process, through presenting the constructs of the design. Hevner observed that *constructs provide the language in which problems and solution are defined and communicated* [6]. Having identified the likely theories/hypotheses that can explain the problem system, and the design principles employed for the class of artifact, the explanatory model can be developed by linking the kernel knowledge and the meta-design principles. This is a creative process on the part of the researcher that requires them to identify how the design principles are linked to the kernel knowledge and define the relationship between the utility requirements, the kernel knowledge, and the meta-design principles [7]. An explanatory model can then be developed which represents from a high level, how the design of the artifact is expected to affect the problem system.

5. Analyze the Artifact to Confirm the Design Principles and Explanatory Model

The artifact can now be systematically analyzed to demonstrate the explanatory model, and how the design principles were instantiated. If it is not possible to review the artifact being investigated then interviews with individuals or groups involved with the design of the artifact can be used to confirm the explanatory model. Any changes discovered through systematic analysis of the artifact will impact steps 3 & 4.

4   The Case of the Irish HSE's EWS Chart

4.1   Background

The National Early Warning Score (NEWS) system was introduced by the HSE in Ireland, with the system being designed to assist with the identification of patients at risk of deterioration. NEWS is a form of aggregate-weighted-track-and-trigger system (AWTTS), where numerical scores are associated with specific patient vital statistics within certain ranges and care protocols are then associated with the calculated aggregate score. In the case of the Irish HSE's version of NEWS, a minimum score of 3 requires elevated care levels for the patient. As well as the score, a key component of the NEWS system is the paper early warning score (EWS) chart on which the patient's vital signs are recorded and on which the scores are shown. When training healthcare professionals (HCPs) to use the NEWS system an emphasis is placed on the HCP to use their own clinical reasoning skills to identify patient deterioration, as it is accepted that the score calculated may not reflect a true picture of the patients health. The design of EWS charts has been found to have an effect on both expert and novice nurses ability to recognize patient deterioration in an accurate and timely manner [8], with nurses being the primary user of EWS charts. However, little documentation exists regarding the design of the Irish HSE's EWS chart, therefore making evaluation of the usefulness of the chart difficult.

In order to develop a coherent and adequately comprehensive understanding of the design process for the HSE's EWS Chart the approach for *RDKS* was employed. This procedural approach outlines methods for identification of knowledge pertaining to each stage of the *process model for procedurally transparent design science research* (PMPT) by Gleasure et al. (2012). Table 1 outlines the knowledge that needs to be discovered before a utilitarian evaluation of the EWS Chart can be performed. The following sections describe the methods used to collect and synthesize this knowledge, as well as an outline of the knowledge collected.

4.2   Step 1: Identify the Utility Requirements

Track and Trigger EWS systems were developed to facilitate the early identification of patients at risk of deterioration, and prediction of adverse clinical outcomes [9].

However, identification of at risk depends on nurses' clinical reasoning skills. When reading vital signs displayed on EWS charts the nurse performs information processing tasks to allow them to interpret the information, thereby forming an initial picture of the patient's state of health [10]. However, prior to development of standard EWS charts, nurses were required to use multiple charts with non-standardized displays, therefore requiring higher levels of cognitive effort on the part of the nurse to interpret the vital statistics [11].

From reviewing of the existing documentation regarding the design of the NEWS systems and a standardized EWS chart it was possible to outline the changes the EWS chart is required to make to the problem system (i.e. improve identification of acute illness in patients), as well as outside the problem system (i.e. facilitate national training). Therefore the problem system can be defined as; 'to *provide easier recognition of patient data, compared to charts currently in use*' and the required change to the problem system can be defined as '*improve support for identification of abnormal clinical parameters*' [11]. As the standardized EWS chart is designed to replace a myriad of charts previously used in hospitals[12], the performance of the EWS chart would have to be compared to charts nurses have used prior to the NEWS EWS chart.

Problem System   • Early Identification of acute illness in patients

Required Changes in   • Provide easier recognition of patient data
Problem System   • Aid identification of abnormal clinical parameters

The following statement can then be made for the utility requirements of the EWS chart: *The EWS Chart should be designed to help early identification of acute illness in patients by providing easier recognition of patient data compared to charts currently in use, and aiding identification of abnormal clinical parameters.*

4.3   Step 2: Identify Kernel Knowledge

The design of the NEWS chart is important as research has established that good design of the chart can have a significant impact on the HCP's ability to recognize abnormal vital signs therefore positively impacting HCPs clinical reasoning skills [8]. Considering this, it is worthwhile establishing the clinical reasoning tasks the design of an EWS chart is likely to impact. In order to establish an adequate coverage of clinical reasoning literature, a systematic literature review is performed. Three leading scientific full-text databases were searched for relevant literature pertaining to nurse clinical reasoning, these were *Science Direct, JSTOR,* and *EBSCO Academic Search Complete* were used to identify relevant literature. *Google Scholar* was also used to track key literature that may not have been available using the previously mentioned databases. This literature search produced 83 results, with further analysis of these papers producing 33 papers relating to how nurses process information as part of clinical reasoning. Disagreements existed within the literature regarding the definition of this aspect of clinical reasoning, with Levett-Jones (1012)[10] describing this as information processing, with the tasks of information processing including *interpreting, discriminating, relating, inferring, matching and predicting.* With other authors describing the process as part of critical thinking *i.e. "a purposeful, self-regulatory judgment which results in interpretations, analysis, evaluation and inference".*

Analysis of the papers identified was performed through developing concept-centric matrix CCM as per Webster (2002)[13]. 4 dominant information-processing tasks and 5 less common tasks which nurses employ when processing information for clinical reasoning. *Fig.* 2 present the results of the CCM, this demonstrates the number of times information-processing tasks were identified in the reviewed literature. From this we can see 4 dominant tasks; *pattern recognition, interpreting cues, matching previous situations,* and *relating information.*

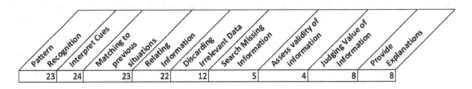

Fig. 2. Results of CCM for key concepts for processing information during clinical reasoning

4.4   Step 3: Establish Meta-design Principles

As the paper-based NEWS system has already been developed, and the design process was not documented, it is not possible to formally establish the design process that was employed to develop the paper-based NEWS chart. By looking at the development of other track and trigger EWS charts we can identify some of the key consideration that impacted the design of the track-and-trigger EWS charts. In order to adequately cover the extant literature regarding track-and-trigger EWS chart design a systematic literature review was performed. The same scientific literature databases use section 5.3 were used for this literature search. This search yielded 68 papers relating to track-and-trigger systems, with review of these papers identifying 12 papers relating to the design of EWS charts for track-and-trigger systems. While only one author was identified who empirically evaluated EWS Chart design to see it's impact on nurse clinical reasoning skills, any paper which made reference to how design principles instantiated in the EWS chart being studied was also included [14, 15]. Furthermore, any literature which visually presented the EWS chart was included as analysis of the chart could be performed to identify design principles instantiated in the chart [8, 14–20].

Based on the articles found, a concept centric matrix (CCM) was developed where relevant concepts to the design of track-and-trigger EWS charts were identified. This process is consistent with that conducted in the previous section 5.3. From analysis of the CCM the following meta-design principles have been identified, which have a direct impact on a HCP's ability to process information presented on track-and-trigger EWS charts. *Fig. 3* presents the results of the CCM, establishing meta-design principles for AWTTS EWS charts.

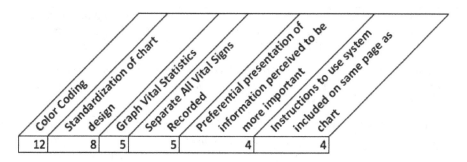

Fig. 3. Results for meta-design principles identified for EWS Chart Design

4.5   Step 4: Develop an Explanatory Model

Based on the utility requirements, kernel knowledge identified, and the meta-design principles identified for AWTTS EWS charts, it is possible to establish that the priorities for the design of the chart were to facilitate interpretation of vital statistics. An explanatory causal model, as represented in *fig. 4* demonstrates how facilitating the interpretation of vital signs should improve clinical decision making for nurses. In this case, interpretation of vital statistics refers to coming to an initial understanding of the patients possible condition based on the vital signs recorded.

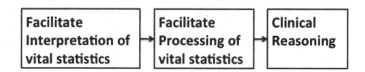

Fig. 4. Predictive model for paper-based NEWS chart

4.6   Step 5: Analyze the Instantiation

By analyzing the EWS Chart and comparing it to the meta-design principles identified for AWTTS EWS charts as a class of artifact, it is possible to establish which design principles have been instantiated in the EWS chart. While not all of the possible design principles identified are apparent in the design of the Irish HSE's EWS chart, the following design principles can be identified on the HSE's EWS Chart:

Design Principles	How Design-Principle Should Impact Problem System
Standardize approach to chart design	*Accurate detection of physiological deterioration is reliant on a chart that is well plotted and indeed in this study training of clinical staff in plotting observations based on defined standards resulted in significant improvements in the quality of the observation chart plot and in detection rates of most parameters.* (Chatterjee, 2005)[21]

Color code vital statistic ranges	*Color can be an effective way of drawing attention to abnormal observations in track-and-trigger systems.* (Preece, 2013) [14]
Graph vital statistics	*Graphical displays of information can in some cases lead to faster and more accurate decision making.* (Baker, 2009) [22]
Graph each vital statistic separately	*Both novice and experienced health professionals responded faster and made fewer errors in classifying observations as normal or abnormal when blood pressure and pulse were presented on separate graphs, rather than over-lapping plots on the same graph.* (Preece, 2012) [15]

5   Discussion and Conclusion

This paper presents an approach that can be taken for reflection on a situated artifact or legacy system to abstract the necessary design knowledge needed to rigorously evaluate the usefulness of the artifact. It was posited that without developing an understanding of the situated artifact and the problem system the artifact was situated in, then it is not possible to develop a coherent data collection method that assesses whether the artifact has caused the desired change in the problem system. By developing an understanding of the problem system and the design principles instantiated in the artifact, then it is possible to reflect on the design of the artifact as per Reymen's definition of reflection: *Reflection on a design process means an introspective contemplation of the designer's perception of the design situation and the remembered design activities* [7, 23].

Adequately reflecting on the design of an artifact allows the individual designing the research to understand who the artifact is designed for, and in turn can establish what data needs to be collected to establish the utility of the artifact [24]. Peffers et al. (2008) made a similar observation, stating that the purpose of artifact evaluation is to *observe and measure how well the artifact supports a solution to the problem. This activity involves comparing the objectives of a solution to actual observed results from use of the artifact in the demonstration.*

Furthermore, the approach for *reflective design knowledge synthesis* (RDKS) also presents an opportunity to add to the body of design knowledge for the class of artifact being investigated. The RDKS approach places an emphasis on systematic and rigorous review of design knowledge for each stage of the design stages of the PMPT model. As such taking the RDKS approach can significantly contribute to the body of knowledge regarding the class of artifact being studied.

This paper also demonstrated how the RDKS approach can be practically implemented through the case of the Irish HSE's EWS Chart used in conjunction with their NEWS system. Using the approach for RDKS, the following design knowledge for the HSE's EWS chart could be formalised:

- The *utility requirements* for the EWS Chart
- The *kernel knowledge* establishes how nurses process vital sign information as part of the clinical reasoning process.
- The *meta-design principles* for the class of artifact being investigated (*EWS Charts for Track-and-Trigger Systems*)
- An *explanatory/predictive model* that explains at a high level how the EWS chart is predicted to impact the problem system
- The design principles instantiated in the HSE's EWS Chart

While this paper outlines how an the approach for RDKS is suitable for discovering design knowledge for a situated artifact, and the paper also shows how the approach can be practically implemented, there is a need for further evaluation of this model. Evaluation of this model is consistent with the design science maxim of demonstrating utility to meet the objectives of the problem system, however in order to discover the generalizability of this approach, there would be a need to evaluate this approach with more cases.

References

1. Järvinen, P.: Action Research is Similar to Design Science. Quality & Quantity 41, 37–54 (2007), doi:10.1007/s11135-005-5427-1
2. Gleasure, R., Feller, J., Flaherty, B.O.: Procedurally Transparent Design Science Research: A Design Process Model. In: Thirty Third International Conference on Information Systems, Orlando, pp. 1–19 (2012)
3. Carlsson, S.A., Henningsson, S., Hrastinski, S., Keller, C.: Socio-technical IS design science research: developing design theory for IS integration management. Information Systems and E-Business Management 9, 109–131 (2011), doi:10.1007/s10257-010-0140-6
4. Walls, J.G., Widmeyer, G.R., El Sawy, O.A.: Building an Information System Design Theory for Vigilant EIS. Information Systems Research 3, 36–59 (1992)
5. Markus, M.L., Majchrzak, A., Gasser, L.: A Design Theory for Systems That Supports Emergent Knowledge Process. MIS Quarterly 26, 179–212 (2002)
6. Hevner, A.R., March, S.T., Park, J., Ram, S.: Design Science in Information Systems Research. MIS Quarterly 28, 75–105 (2004)
7. Gregor, S., Müller, O., Seidel, S.: Reflection, Abstraction And Theorizing In Design And Development Research. In: ECIS 2013 Completed Research. Paper 74 (2013)
8. Preece, M.H.W., Hill, A., Horswill, M.S., Watson, M.O.: Supporting the detection of patient deterioration: observation chart design affects the recognition of abnormal vital signs. Resuscitation 83, 1111–1118 (2012), doi:10.1016/j.resuscitation.2012.02.009
9. Smith, G.B., Prytherch, D.R., Schmidt, P.E., Featherstone, P.I.: Review and performance evaluation of aggregate weighted " track and trigger " systems. Resuscitation 77, 170–179 (2008), doi:10.1016/j.resuscitation.2007.12.004
10. Levett-Jones, T., Hoffman, K., Dempsey, J., et al.: The "Five rights" of clinical reasoning: an educational model to enhance nursing students' ability to identify and manage clinically "at risk" patients. Nurse education today 30, 515–520 (2010), doi:10.1016/j.nedt.2009.10.020
11. Royal College of Physicians, National Early Warning Score (NEWS) Standardising the assessment of acute-illness severity in the NHS. 29 (2012)

12. McGinley, A., Pearse, R.M.: A national early warning score for acutely ill patients. Bmj 5310, e5310–e5310 (2012), doi:10.1136/bmj.e5310

13. Webster, B.J., Watson, R.T., Webster, J.: Analyzing the past to prepare for the future: Writing a literature review. MIS Quarterly 26 (2002)

14. Preece, M.H.W., Hill, A., Horswill, M.S., et al.: Applying heuristic evaluation to observation chart design to improve the detection of patient deterioration. Applied ergonomics 44, 544–556 (2013), doi:10.1016/j.apergo.2012.11.003

15. Preece, M.H.W., Hill, A., Horswill, M.S., et al.: Designing observation charts to optimize the detection of patient deteriorioation: reliance on the subjective preferences of healthcare professionals is not enough. Australian Critical Care: Official Journal of the Confederation of Australian Critical Care Nurses 25, 238–252 (2012), doi:10.1016/j.aucc.2012.01.003

16. Preece, M.H.W., Horswill, M.S., Hill, A., Watson, M.O.: The Development of the Adult Deterioration Detection System (ADDS) Chart (2010)

17. Horswill, M.S., Preece, M.H.W., Hill, A., et al.: Recording patient data on six observation charts: An experimental comparison (2010)

18. Mitchell, I.A., McKay, H., Van Leuvan, C., et al.: A prospective controlled trial of the effect of a multi-faceted intervention on early recognition and intervention in deteriorating hospital patients. Resuscitation 81, 658–666 (2010), doi:10.1016/j.resuscitation.2010.03.001

19. Cahill, H., Jones, A., Herkes, R., et al.: Introduction of a new observation chart and education programme is associated with higher rates of vital-sign ascertainment in hospital wards. BMJ quality & safety 20, 791–796 (2011), doi:10.1136/bmjqs.2010.045096

20. Jones, M.: NEWSDIG: The National Early Warning Score Development and Implementation Group. Clinical medicine 12, 501–503 (2012)

21. Chatterjee, M.T., Moon, J.C., Murphy, R., McCrea, D.: The "OBS" chart: an evidence based approach to re-design of the patient observation chart in a district general hospital setting. Postgraduate Medical Journal 81, 663–666 (2005), doi:10.1136/pgmj.2004.031872

22. Baker, J., Burkman, J., Jones, D.R.: Using Visual Representations of Data to Enhance Sensemaking in Data Exploration Tasks. Journal of the Association for Information Systems 10, 533–559 (2009)

23. Reymen, I.: Improving design processes through structured reflection: A domain-independent approach. Technische Universiteit Eindhoven (2001)

24. Jan Baskerville, P.-H., Baskerville, R., Venable, J.R., Pries-Heje, J.: Strategies for Design Science Research Evaluation. In: European Conference on Information Systems (ECIS), p. 87 (2008)

25. Peffers, K., Tuunanen, T., Rothenberger, M.A., Chatterjee, S.: A Design Science Research Methodology for Information Systems Research. Journal of Management Information Systems 24, 45–77 (2008), doi:10.2753/MIS0742-1222240302

Design Thinking and Evaluation Using an Ontology

Arkalgud Ramaprasad[1,2] and Thant Syn[1]

[1] University of Miami, Coral Gables, Florida, USA
{prasad,thant}@miami.edu
[2] University of Illinois at Chicago, Chicago, Illinois, USA
prasad@uic.edu

Abstract. We present the use of an ontology as a tool for thinking about the idealized design of a system and the evaluation of the realized design. The ontology concisely encapsulates the logic of the system. It can be used to think through all the potential components of the system in a natural language. By mapping the actual requirements on to the ontology one can highlight the gaps between the idealized and realized designs and evaluate them. Thus, it will help recognize the logical coherence or lack of it in the design. The paper describes the method of (a) logically constructing an ontology, (b) thinking about the design, and (c) evaluating the design. We illustrate the method with its application to the multi-stage design for enhancing the meaningful use of healthcare information systems in USA by its Center for Medicaid and Medicare Services (CMS).

Keywords: design thinking, design evaluation, ontology, meaningful use.

1 Introduction

Design problems can be large, complex, and ill-structured – they can be 'wicked' [1]. Iterative formulation, evaluation, feedback, and learning are necessary for the thinking about the design to evolve rapidly and the design to converge to a few plausible alternatives. For effective iteration of thinking and evaluation, we need a comprehensive framework and method for abstraction and application [2, 3]. It is necessary to avoid replaying the proverbial story of the five blind men each of whom imagined an elephant as a rock, an arrow, a fan, a rope, and a tree trunk after touching its body, tusk, ear, tail, and leg respectively [4, 5]. A wise man settles their argument about the nature of the elephant by piecing together the picture for them. Fortuitously, the wise man in the story could see and recognize the elephant; he could help the blind men 'see' the elephant. Analogously we need a tool which can help designers think about a problem and evaluate the design alternatives comprehensively. The tool should (a) minimize the fragmentation of the design, (b) make the whole design greater than the sum of its parts, and (c) help solve the problem systemically and systematically. It should also be adaptable to the subsequent evolution of the problem through scaling, extension, reduction, refinement, and magnification of its components. In this paper, we will present an ontology [5] as a tool for design thinking and evaluation.

M. Helfert et al. (Eds.): EDSS 2013, CCIS 447, pp. 63–74, 2014.

We will illustrate design thinking and evaluation using an ontology by applying it to the design of a national program to promote meaningful use of healthcare information systems (MUHIS) in the USA. MUHIS is essential to manage the cost, quality, safety, and accessibility of healthcare. The escalating costs of healthcare on the one hand and the increasing expectations of its outcomes on the other make it essential to deliver the care effectively and efficiently. The rapid developments in information technology offer the promise of transforming health and healthcare if, and only if, systems can be deployed meaningfully to transport the necessary information among the stakeholders and translate the system solutions into meaningful practice [6]. MUHIS requirements and practices are evolving in tandem and they have to do so quickly to fulfill the rapidly increasing demands on healthcare. To catalyze their evolution the Centers for Medicaid & Medicare Services (CMS) in the USA has set Stages 1 and 2 meaningful use requirements for Electronic Health Records (EHR) [7]. The requirements specify the outcomes, associated objectives, and corresponding measures. There are incentives for meeting the objectives. The challenge of designing and evaluating MUHIS is large, complex, and ill-structured.

In the following, we will (a) describe the construction of the ontology (idealized design), (b) its application to design thinking, (c) mapping the MUHIS requirements (realized design), and (d) evaluate the gaps between the two designs. We will conclude with a brief discussion of ad-hoc, rational, and pragmatic design thinking strategies as possible explanations of the gaps.

2   Ontology of MUHIS

Ontologies represent the conceptualization of a domain [8]; they organize the terminologies and taxonomies of a domain. An ontology is an "explicit specification of a conceptualization." [9, p. 908] It is used to systematize the description of a complex system [10]. "Our acceptance of an ontology is… similar in principle to our acceptance of a scientific theory, say a system of physics; we adopt, at least insofar as we are reasonable, the simplest conceptual scheme into which the disordered fragments of raw experience can be fitted and arranged." [11, p. 16]While automated ontology extraction tools such as OWL [12] are available, they cannot yet formulate an ontology which is parsimonious and organized such that the components can be concatenated as natural language sentences. These tools are designed for standardizing terminologies, as for example in Medicine, but not to extract semantically valid sentences describing the components of the system [13].

Our method of constructing the ontology shown in Fig. 1 is based on Ramaprasad and Mitroff's framework [2, 3] for formulating ill-structured problems; it is in turn based on the model proposed by Piaget [14] for understanding causality. It starts with an initial problem statement (left top corner) – in the present case 'meaningful use of healthcare information systems.' The final ontology is shown in Fig. 2. The initial problem elements are abstracted from the domain based on the literature and personal knowledge through Data Abstraction (DA). DA would include, in our example, the connotations of 'meaningful use' and 'healthcare information systems'. We drew largely upon the CMS connotations of these terms [6, 7].

The initial ontology (top level) is informed by the problem statement, the corresponding elements, and the associated body of knowledge. For example: the deconstruction of healthcare information systems into the Structure and Function dimensions, and their corresponding taxonomies, is in keeping with the common body of knowledge in information systems. However, the deconstruction of meaningful use into the Management, Stakeholder, and Outcome dimensions required a few iterations.

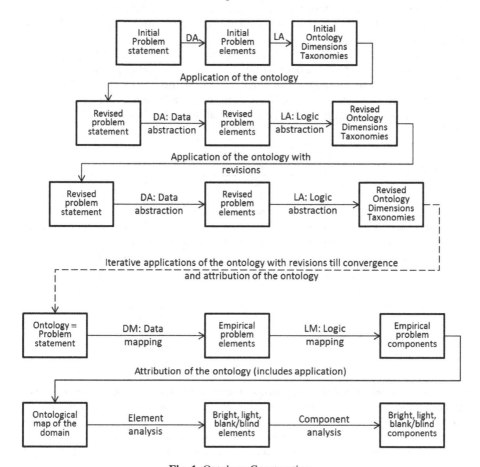

Fig. 1. Ontology Construction

The next step is to extract the logic underlying these elements (LA: Logic abstraction in Fig. 1) by (a) grouping related elements into problem dimensions, (b) the elements within each dimension into taxonomies, and (c) organizing the dimensions left to right with suitable connecting words and phrases so that the concatenation of elements across the columns is a natural English sentence (Fig. 2). Four illustrative sentences, each representing a component of MUHIS, are shown at the bottom of Fig. 2. There are 6*4*5*7*4 = 3360 such concatenations encapsulated in the figure. They represent the core logic of MUHIS.

The process of ontological analysis is iterative as shown in the top three layers in Fig. 1. It is similar to the Generate/Test Cycle [15].An initial ontology is formulated, applied to the problem statement (which is revised, if necessary), the data and the logic are re-abstracted, and the ontology revised. The cycle is repeated till there is a convergence of the problem statement, elements, logic, and the ontology. The ontology should encapsulate the problem statement, the elements, and the problem logic. It should also be complete. Thus, for example, even though insurers are not identified as stakeholders in the CMS requirements, they are integral to MUHIS and therefore included in the framework.

In the last stage of ontology construction (bottom layer of Fig. 1) the ontology is attributed to the problem, from being applied to it as in the earlier phases. The ontology becomes the problem statement; it is not 'as if' it is the statement. It is also a visualization of the problem statement. Subsequent to the attribution, the data and logic can be mapped to the ontology, instead of being abstracted to develop it.

Healthcare Information Systems

Management		Structure		Function		Stakeholders		Outcome	
Analysis	[of]	Technology	[for]	Acquisition	[of information by/to]	Recipients	[to meaningfully manage]	Efficiency	[of/in healthcare]
Specification		Hardware		Analysis		Patients		Quality	
Design		Software		Interpretation		Families		Safety	
Implementation		Networks		Application		Population		Disparities	
Maintenance		Processes		Distribution		Providers			
Assessment		Policies				Physicians			
		Personnel				Nurses			
						Pharmacists			
						Payers			
						Employers			
						Insurers			
						Regulators			
						Government			

Four Illustrative components of meaningful use of HIS from 3360 (6x4x5x7x4) level-1 components:
1. Specification of technology for analysis of information by providers to meaningfully manage cost of healthcare.
   Examples: electronic health records software, data mining software
2. Design of processes for acquisition of information by patients to meaningfully manage quality of healthcare.
   Examples: access to online lab results, formation of social networks
3. Implementation of policies for application of information by government to meaningfully manage disparities in healthcare.
   Examples: wellness education policies, Medicaid reimbursement policies
4. Implementation (deployment) of personnel for interpretation of information by insurers to meaningfully manage safety of healthcare.
   Examples: data mining specialists

Fig. 2. Ontology of meaningful use of healthcare information systems (MUHIS)

3   Design Thinking

The ontology can be used as a tool to think about the idealized design [16] logically, systematically, and systemically. At the core of such thinking is the question: Does the ontology encapsulate the logic of the system being designed? To answer this question we have to answer two other questions: (a) Are there errors of omission – exclusion of items which should be included? (b) Are their errors of commission – inclusion of items which should be excluded? These questions may be posed with respect to (a) the dimensions (columns) of the ontology, (b) the taxonomies of the dimensions, and (c) the components derived by the concatenation of the dimensions.

3.1   Dimensions (Columns) of the Ontology

The dimensions of the ontology have to be parsimonious yet comprehensive. Too many dimensions will increase the complexity of design exponentially; too few dimensions, on the other hand, may specify the problem partially or incorrectly. The five dimensions of the MUHIS ontology in Fig. 2 were derived from the deconstruction of the problem statement and the extant domain knowledge. It is a specification, not <u>the</u> specification of the problem. A different set of dimensions will result in a different perspective on the problem [13] .

Consider, for example, the Stakeholders dimension. The inclusion of this dimension compels the consideration of meaningful use from the perspective of the different stakeholders individually. Meaningful use for a Provider, for example, may be very different from that for a Recipient, or an Insurer. In thinking about the design, one has to explicitly accommodate these different points of view. On the other hand, if the Stakeholders dimension was eliminated, the thinking would likely be in the aggregate about all stakeholders and not refined with reference to particular stakeholders.

In contrast, for example, consider potential dimensions such as Time and Location which have not been included. The Time dimension could be used to specify the timeframe of meaningful use – for example: Short term, Medium term, and Long term. The Location dimension could be used to specify the location of meaningful use – for example: City, State, Region, and Country. The exclusion of these dimensions diminishes the attention given to these aspects of meaningful use. Should they be important to another designer, they could be added. However, they are not salient in the extant literature.

The dimensions can be extended or reduced as the design thinking evolves. Any change however has to balance the opposing requirements of parsimony and comprehensiveness.

3.2   Taxonomies of Dimensions

The categories of each taxonomy have to be exhaustive, at least within the defined scope of the problem. The exclusion of a significant category will be an error of omission; the inclusion of a non-significant category will be an error of commission. In the United Kingdom, for example, the inclusion of Employer as a stakeholder may not be necessary because of the nationalized healthcare system; but the category has to be included in the USA where employers bear a significant portion of the healthcare costs. Similarly, the exclusion of Assessment in the Management dimension could be a significant error of omission for it would diminish the focus on ongoing feedback and learning necessary for the development of the system.

The ordering of the categories in a taxonomy should reflect the underlying logic of the dimension. Thus, for example, the categories of Management and Function are presented in the ordinal order of their occurrence generally. The categories of Outcome may be nominally ordered (that is, in no particular order), or ordered ordinally based on the designer's priority. In the latter case, explicating the logic of the order can have an important bearing on design thinking. Thus, for example, the implications of Efficiency dominating Quality could be very different from Quality dominating Efficiency. Similarly, the Stakeholders could be ordered ordinally or by their significance to the design. The design with Providers receiving the highest priority could be substantially different from one with the Recipients receiving the highest priority.

The granularity of the categories can be refined by adding subcategories and coarsened by aggregating categories. Thus, for example, the granularity of Providers has been refined by including the subcategories of Physicians, Nurses, and Pharmacists; it could be coarsened by eliminating the subcategories. Similarly, in the Structure dimension we have included Technology as a category with Hardware, Software, and Networks as subcategories. A few years ago the three subcategories would have been considered categories of structure in their own right. However, the emerging crossover functionalities of the three and the consequent blurring of the lines between them would justify considering them as a part of Technology, not independently.

Thus, like the dimensions, the taxonomies can be extended or reduced, coarsened or refined, to match the granularity and complexity of design thinking. The ontology can help the designer zoom in and zoom out without loss of information. The designer can take a macro-, meso-, or micro-level view of the problem.

3.3 Components of the System

All the potential components of the system can be articulated by concatenating all the natural-language sentences like the four illustrative ones shown in Fig. 2. There are 3360 level-1 components of the ontology shown in the figure; there are 7,920 level-2 components. The ability to concisely represent these components makes the ontology a convenient tool for design thinking. All the possible components may neither be necessary nor feasible in the design of the system. Using the ontology one can enumerate (a) the most important components of the system, (b) the less important components, and (c) the infeasible components. Since the ontology itself is a complete, closed description of the system it can serve as a structured brainstorming tools for the designers – compelling them to consider and think through the exclusion or inclusion of all the potential components, at least synoptically if not sequentially (which may take a long time). It can reduce both errors of omission and commission in the design of the system.

Consider the four illustrative components and the examples of each shown at the bottom of Fig. 2:

1. Specification of technology for analysis of information by providers to meaningfully manage cost of healthcare. Examples: electronic health records software, data mining software

2. Design of processes for acquisition of information by patients to meaningfully manage quality of healthcare. Examples: access to online lab results, formation of social networks
3. Implementation of policies for application of information by government to meaningfully manage disparities in healthcare. Examples: wellness education policies, Medicaid reimbursement policies
4. Implementation (deployment) of personnel for interpretation of information by insurers to meaningfully manage safety of healthcare. Examples: data mining specialists

These are instantiable components. Each component of the ontology may be (a) instantiated in many ways (as in #1, 2, and 3), (b) instantiated in a singular way (as in #4), (c) not instantiated at all, or (d) not possible to instantiate. The distinction between those components which are not instantiated and those which cannot be instantiated is important. The former represents a design choice; the latter a design constraint. For example, consider: implementation of processes for distribution of information by insurers to meaningfully mange safety of healthcare. If the insurer has the necessary safety information than the component would be instantiable; on the other hand, if they do not have the information because the provider will not share the same, then the component cannot be instantiated. Once the components of the system are articulated it can focus the designer to think about how, if at all, it can be instantiated.

3.4   Conclusion about Design Thinking

We have discussed how the ontology can be used as a tool to think about the design logically, systemically, and systematically. The advantage of the ontology is that it can make the invisible 'elephant' – the system being designed – visible and articulable in a natural language. Thus the thinking can be made accessible not only to the experts about the system who may have deep knowledge of the system but also the novices, like users, who may have only a passing knowledge of the system but deep knowledge of the requirements. In the next section we will discuss how the ontology can be used for design evaluation, the complement of design thinking.

4   Design Evaluation

We will discuss the MUHIS design evaluation using the Medicare and Medicaid EHR Incentive Programs objectives. These national programs represent a major push by the US for the national adoption of EHR in particular, and through it HIS in general [7]. The following summarizes the program.

> "The Medicare and Medicaid EHR Incentive Programs provide financial incentives for the "meaningful use" of certified EHR technology to improve patient care. To receive an EHR incentive payment, providers have to show that they are "meaningfully using" their EHRs by meeting thresholds for a number of objectives. CMS has established the objectives for "meaningful use" that eligible professionals, eligible hospitals, and critical access hospitals (CAHs) must meet in order to receive an incentive payment."

"The Medicare and Medicaid EHR Incentive Programs are staged in three steps with increasing requirements for participation. All providers begin participating by meeting the Stage 1 requirements for a 90-day period in their first year of meaningful use and a full year in their second year of meaningful use. After meeting the Stage 1 requirements, providers will then have to meet Stage 2 requirements for two full years. Eligible professionals participate in the program on the calendar years, while eligible hospitals and CAHs participate according to the federal fiscal year." [7]

In Stage 1 to qualify for incentive payment eligible professionals have to meet 20 of 25 objectives. The 20 include 15 required core objectives and 5 chosen from a menu of 10 objectives. Eligible hospitals and CAHs have to meet 19 of 24 objectives – 14 core and 5 from a menu of 10. In Stage 2 eligible professionals "must meet 17 core objectives and 3 menu objectives that they select from a total list of 6, or a total of 20 core objectives....Eligible hospitals and CAHs must meet 16 core objectives and 3 menu objectives that they select from a total list of 6, or a total of 19 core objectives." The full set of Stage 1 and Stage 2 objectives are available at CMS.gov [7].

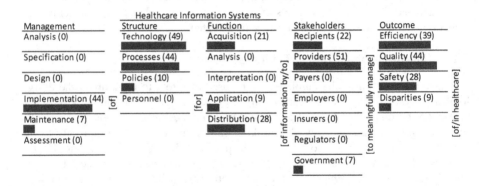

Fig. 3. Meaningful Use of EHR Stages 1 & 2 Objectives

4.1   Mapping the Stages 1 and 2 Objectives

The Stages 1 and 2 objectives implicitly encapsulate the requirements of MUHIS. To evaluate the design for MUHIS as specified these objectives we mapped all the Stages 1 and 2 objectives onto the ontology through consensus coding. All the objectives were first coded by one author, reviewed and modified by the other, and the discrepancies between the two discussed and resolved in the final coding.

The coding does not distinguish between the core and menu objectives, and those for eligible professionals, eligible hospitals, and CAHs. We provide two examples of coding in the following.

Consider the Stage 1 core objective of "Implement drug-drug and drug-allergy interaction checks." It is one of a set of objectives with the stated outcome of "Improving quality, safety, efficiency, and reducing health disparities." We coded the objective for quality, safety, and efficiency outcomes but not for disparities; we could not see a direct link from the discussion of the objective and its measures to managing disparities. We mapped it to the ontology as: "Implementation of technology/processes for application of information by providers to meaningfully manage efficiency/quality/safety." We note that the objective corresponds to six components of the ontology, not just one.

Consider the Stage 2 core objective of "Provide patients the ability to view online, download and transmit their health information within four business days of the information being available to the EP." Although the stated outcome of the objective is "Patient Electronic Access", we inferred the ultimate outcome to be primarily quality. It could be efficiency and safety too, but we did not find sufficient evidence to justify them. We mapped the objective to the ontology as: "Implementation of technology for distribution of information by/to recipients/providers to meaningfully manage quality." Again, we note that the objective corresponds to two components of the ontology.

Coding the meaningful use of EHR objectives was straightforward in most cases. It required little interpretation except in the coding the outcomes of a few objectives as illustrated above. The coding was recorded on an Excel spreadsheet using one row per objective and a column per element of the ontology. Since an objective can be coded into multiple components in the ontology the total number of components encoded exceeds the number of objectives.

The results are shown in the ontology in Fig. 3. The text elements of the map are the same as the level-1 elements in the ontology (Fig. 2). The number in parenthesis adjacent to the element is the frequency of its occurrence in the set of objectives. The bar below the element is proportional to the frequency using the maximum occurrence among all items as the denominator. The profile is very similar for Stages 1 and 2 objectives considered individually and hence they are not shown individually. The total for elements in a column may exceed the total number of CMS objectives due to one to many mapping of objectives to components as illustrated and explained earlier.

4.2   Evaluation of Stages 1 and 2 Objectives

The mapping in Fig. 3 clearly highlights the categories of the ontology which are heavily emphasized in the objectives, those which are lightly emphasized, and those which are not emphasized at all. For example, Implementation, Technology, Processes, and Quality are heavily emphasized; Maintenance, Policies, and Application are lightly emphasized; and Interpretation, Employers, and Regulators are not emphasized at all.

Consider the Stage 1 objective: 'Implement drug-drug and drug-allergy interaction checks'. These checks will directly affect the Quality and Safety[17-19] Outcomes of healthcare[20]. Their effectiveness will depend upon the providers' response to the alerts issued based on the checks. Recent Assessment shows that more than 90% of the alerts are overridden due to alert fatigue[17, 21, 22], information overload[23], poor user interface Design[18, 24, 25], poor Specification of the critical interactions[25], and inadequate Analysis[26, 27] of the interactions. It will be necessary to include most of the blank elements in the topography of Stages 1 and 2 (Figure 2) to improve the effectiveness of the checks. First, it would be necessary to Assess[28, 29] the current system to provide feedback[21] for Analysis[26, 27],

Specification, and Design of the system. Second, the Assessment could be done internally by a provider, locally, or by a conference of all the Stakeholders [22, 26, 30]. Third, any Assessment and feedback will entail extensive Analysis[26, 27] and Interpretation[31] of empirical data[32]. Thus, the success of a large number of components encapsulated in the ontology will be essential for effectively implementing the 'drug-drug and drug-allergy interaction checks'. In absence of a systematic systemic [28] perspective, the checks may be implemented but they may be meaningless, especially if they are overridden constantly[33].

The ontology in Fig. 2 is an idealized [16] portrait of MUHIS. It is the logical articulation of MUHIS. By contrast, the mapping of objectives in Fig. 3 is the realized design, at least in so far as the Stages 1 and 2 are concerned. The gaps between the two are many and large. They may be consequence of (a) ad-hoc design, (b) rational design, or (c) pragmatic design. We will discuss the three in the conclusion.

5   Conclusion

The gaps between the idealized and realized designs may be symptomatic of the 'five blind men and the elephant' syndrome [4, 5]. It may be a consequence of fragmentation fostered by the absence of a systemic framework and a systematic approach. The wide variation in emphases may be indicative of the 'narrow' perspectives of the designers involved. On the other hand, it may also be a product of rational design. The designers may have deliberately chosen the emphases. Such a choice would be surprising, for it flies in the face of extant evidence, as discussed in the context of drug-drug and drug-allergy interaction. Last, it may also be a product of pragmatic design. It may simply be the entry point for MUHIS – only a hook to get the Providers and Recipients engaged, and to set the ball rolling. If so, the emphases can be interpreted as the strategic points of entry for MUHIS with the intent of subsequently expanding to the other components. The staged introduction of requirements may give some credence to this possibility.

Irrespective of the reason for the gaps, the ontology provides a systemic and systematic framework for thinking about and evaluating the design. We have illustrated the application in the context of MUHIS, but the method can be extended to other domains and systems.

References

1. Churchman, C.W.: Wicked Problems. Management Science 14, B 141 (1967)
2. Ramaprasad, A.: Cognitive Process as a Basis for MIS and DSS Design. Management Science 33, 139–148 (1987)
3. Ramaprasad, A., Mitroff, I.I.: On Formulating Strategic Problems. Acad Manage Rev. 9, 597–605 (1984)
4. Börner, K., Chen, C., Boyack, K.W.: Visualizing knowledge domains. Annual Review of Information Science and Technology 37, 179–255 (2003)
5. Ramaprasad, A., Papagari, S.S.: Ontological Design. In: Proceedings of DESRIST 2009, Malvern, PA (2009)
6. http://www.healthit.gov/providers-professionals

7. https://www.cms.gov/Regulations-and-Guidance/Legislation/
   EHRIncentivePrograms/Meaningful_Use.html
8. Gruber, T.R.: Ontology. In: Liu, L., Ozsu, M.T. (eds.) Encyclopedia of Database Systems, Springer (2008)
9. Gruber, T.R.: Toward Principles for the Design of Ontologies Used for Knowledge Sharing. International Journal Human-Computer Studies 43, 907–928 (1995)
10. Cimino, J.J.: In defense of the Desiderata. Journal of Biomedical Informatics 39, 299–306 (2006)
11. Quine, W.V.O.: From a Logical Point of View. Harvard University Press, Boston (1961)
12. OWL 2 Web Ontology Language, vol. 2013 May 2, (2012, 2013),
    http://www.w3.org/TR/2012/REC-owl2-overview-20121211/ (retrieved)
13. Ramaprasad, A., Syn, T.: Ontological Meta-Analysis and Synthesis. In: Proceedings of the Nineteenth Americas Conference on Information Systems, August 15-17. Chicago, Illinois (2013)
14. Piaget, J.: Understanding Causality. Norton, New York (1974)
15. Hevner, A.R., March, S.T., Park, J., Ram, S.: Design science in information systems research. MIS Quarterly 28, 75–105 (2004)
16. Ackoff, R.L., Magidson, J., Addison, H.J.: Idealized design: How to dissolve tomorrow's crisis. Wharton School Publishing (2006)
17. Crosson, J.C., Schueth, A.J., Isaacson, N., Bell, D.S.: Early adopters of electronic prescribing struggle to make meaningful use of formulary checks and medication history documentation. The Journal of the American Board of Family Medicine 25, 24–32 (2012)
18. Rahmner, P.B., Eiermann, B., Korkmaz, S., Gustafsson, L.L., Gruvén, M., Maxwell, S., Eichle, H.-G., Vég, A.: Physicians' reported needs of drug information at point of care in Sweden. British Journal of Clinical Pharmacology 73, 115–125 (2012)
19. Spina, J.R., Glassman, P.A., Simon, B., Lanto, A., Lee, M., Cunningham, F., Good, C.B.: Potential Safety Gaps in Order Entry and Automated Drug Alerts: A Nationwide Survey of VA Physician Self-Reported Practices With Computerized Order Entry. Medical Care 49, 904–910 (2011)
20. Classen, D.C., Phansalkar, S., Bates, D.W.: Critical drug-drug interactions for use in electronic health records systems with computerized physician order entry: review of leading approaches. Journal of Patient Safety 7, 61–65 (2011)
21. Smithburger, P.L., Buckley, M.S., Bejian, S., Burenheide, K., Kane-Gill, S.L.: A critical evaluation of clinical decision support for the detection of drug-drug interactions. Expert Opinion on Drug Safety 10, 871–882 (2011)
22. Phansalkar, S., van der Sijs, H., Tucker, A.D., Desai, A.A., Bell, D.S., Teich, J.M., Middleton, B., Bates, D.W.: Drug–drug interactions that should be non-interruptive in order to reduce alert fatigue in electronic health records. Journal of the American Medical Informatics Association (2012)
23. Callen, J.L., Westbrook, J.I., Georgiou, A., Li, J.: Failure to Follow-Up Test Results for Ambulatory Patients: A Systematic Review. Journal of General Internal Medicine 27, 1334–1348 (2011)
24. Seidling, H.M., Phansalkar, S., Seger, D.L., Paterno, M.D., Shaykevich, S., Haefeli, W.E., Bates, D.W.: Factors influencing alert acceptance: a novel approach for predicting the success of clinical decision support. Journal of the American Medical Informatics Association 18, 479–484 (2011)
25. Gaikwad, R., Sketris, I., Shepherd, M., Duffy, J.: Evaluation of accuracy of drug interaction alerts triggered by two electronic medical record systems in primary healthcare. Health Informatics Journal 13, 163–177 (2007)

26. Phansalkar, S., Desai, A.A., Bell, D., Yoshida, E., Doole, J., Czochanski, M., Middleton, B., Bates, D.W.: High-priority drug–drug interactions for use in electronic health records. Journal of the American Medical Informatics Association 19, 735–743 (2012)
27. Takarabe, M., Shigemizu, D., Kotera, M., Goto, S., Kanehisa, M.: Network-Based Analysis and Characterization of Adverse Drug–Drug Interactions. Journal of Chemical Information and Modeling 51, 2977–2985 (2011)
28. Saverno, K.R., Hines, L.E., Warholak, T.L., Grizzle, A.J., Babits, L., Clark, C., Taylor, A.M., Malone, D.C.: Ability of pharmacy clinical decision-support software to alert users about clinically important drug–drug interactions. Journal of the American Medical Informatics Association 18, 32–37 (2011)
29. Warholak, T.L., Hines, L.E., Saverno, K.R., Grizzle, A.J., Malone, D.C.: Assessment tool for pharmacy drug–drug interaction software. Journal of the American Pharmacists Association 51, 418–424 (2011)
30. Hines, L.E., Malone, D.C., Murphy, J.E.: Recommendations for Generating, Evaluating, and Implementing Drug - Drug Interaction Evidence. Pharmacotherapy: The Journal of Human Pharmacology and Drug Therapy 32, 304–313 (2012)
31. Dhabali, A.A.H., Awang, R., Zyoud, S.H.: Clinically important drug–drug interactions in primary care. Journal of Clinical Pharmacy and Therapeutics (2012)
32. Haueis, P., Greil, W., Huber, M., Grohmann, R., Kullak-Ublick, G.A., Russmann, S.: Evaluation of drug interactions in a large sample of psychiatric inpatients: a data interface for mass analysis with clinical decision support software. Clinical Pharmacology & Therapeutics 90, 588–596 (2011)
33. Yu, D.T., Seger, D.L., Lasser, K.E., Karson, A.S., Fiskio, J.M., Seger, A.C., Bates, D.W.: Impact of implementing alerts about medication black-box warnings in electronic health records. Pharmacoepidemiology and Drug Safety 20, 192–202 (2011)

Applying Design Thinking
throughout the Product Lifecycle in Dell Inc.

Rick Menchaca[1], Niall Donnellan[1], Glenn Wintrich[1], and Brian Donnellan[2]

[1] Dell Computer Corporation, One Dell Way, Round Rock, Texas 78682
{Rick_Menchaca,Niall_Donnellan,Glenn_Wintrich}@dell.com
[2] Innovation Value Institute, National University of Ireland, Maynooth
Brian.Donnellan@nuim.ie

Abstract. Customer/human-centered design can positively affect insight and idea generation in a natural and meaningful way by helping operations team members review chronic or open-ended problems with a new lens. Dell's experience has been consistent with other organizations in that Design Thinking as a methodology can be applied to many problem spaces to generate innovative solutions. This paper examines cases studies of the application of Design Thinking in Dell in the context of current thinking in Design Thinking in the academic and practitioner communities.

Keywords: Design Thinking, Design research, Information System, Practice.

1   Introduction

Customer/human-centred design can positively affect insight and idea generation in a natural and meaningful way by helping operations team members review chronic or open-ended problems with a new lens. Dell's experience has been consistent with other organizations that Design Thinking as a methodology can be applied to many problem spaces to come up with innovative solutions. Our goal in this paper is to explore the application of Design Thinking in Dell Inc. In Section 2 we provide an academic introduction to the topic and an overview of Design Thinking. Section 3 then provides a description of the context of this work in Dell Inc. Section 4 describes the application of Design Thinking in Dell using three practical examples. Section 5 summarizes the conclusions to be drawn from our work.

2   Background to Design Research and Innovation

Research in design has a long history in many fields including architecture, engineering, education, psychology and the fine arts [4]. Bannon [3] points out that the Bauhaus laid the foundation for what we today think of as modern design - 'useful', functionalist, transparent objects of design: buildings, furniture and utensils, combining traditional materials like glass and leather with 'modern' materials like steel and reinforced concrete and, later, plastic composite materials and information

M. Helfert et al. (Eds.): EDSS 2013, CCIS 447, pp. 75–87, 2014.

technology. The Bauhaus was inspired by the notion of the Bauhiitten - the medieval organization of craftspeople involved in building cathedrals, except that the Bauhaus was more about the cathedral of the future - that is, mundane objects that would support people in their everyday, secularized life. It was collaborative and interdisciplinary, joining the different design competences of art, craft, architecture and technology - in order to build a Gesamtkunstwerk, a genuinely collaborative design work. The foundation for this work was the collaborative building activities that took place in the Bauhaus workshops.

Efeoglu et al. [9] provide a comprehensive review of types of Design Thinking – covering (i) Circular Approaches, (ii) Sequential Approaches and (iii) Other approaches:

(i) Circular Approaches
- Brown's method comprises three core steps: Inspiration, Ideation and Implementation. [5].
- Dunne and Martin's [8] approach consists of inductive, deductive and abductive elements. While induction and deduction are comparable to the divergence and convergence of the thinking process, abductive logic generates truly new ideas. Ideas are then tested in practice.

(ii) Sequential Approaches
- Stanford D School method is a sequential approach with multiple phases. This approach categorizes the phases into a problem and a solution space. The problem space comprises the phases: understand, observe and point of view. The solution space comprises the ideate, prototype and test phases.[14]

(iii) Other Approaches
- The University of St. Gallen has developed a circular design thinking interpretation based on Stanford's d.school approach. While the St. Gallen approach does not mention any problem and solution spaces there is a pattern noticeable. The problem space also includes need finding, while the remainder belongs to the solution space [14].

Design Thinking, has become a central issue in **modern** design discourse and rhetoric. Kelly's [12] influential book on Design Thinking has had a significant impact on companies such as IDEO. Verganti [18] addresses Design-Driven Innovation as being "about how to manage innovation that customers do not expect but eventually love. It shows how executives can realize an innovation strategy that leads to products and services that have a radical new meaning: those that convey a completely new reason for customers to buy them. Their meanings are so distinct from those that dominate the market that they might take people by surprise, but they are so inevitable that they convert people and make them passionate." He calls this strategy "design-driven innovation" because design, in its etymological sense, means "making sense of things" and he is concerned about "how companies can manage this process to radically overturn dominant meanings in an industry before their competitors so and therefore rule the competitors."

Today, design activities are central to most applied disciplines. The ICT field, since its advent in the late 1940's has appropriated many of the ideas, concepts, and methods of Design that have originated in these other disciplines. However, information systems (IS) as composed of inherently mutable and adaptable hardware, software, and human interfaces provide many unique and challenging design problems that call for new and creative ideas, e.g. innovations. The voluminous and eclectic innovation literature has been described by Adams et al. [1] as a "fragmented corpus." In an antecedent paper, Wolfe [20] concluded that it had made little contribution to the understanding of innovative behavior in organizations and his evaluation of the results as being "inconclusive, inconsistent and characterized by low levels of explanation" was surely a pointed criticism of the field. Slappendel's [15] subsequent mapping of the literature on innovation in organizations in terms of three theoretical regions; the individualist perspective, the structuralist perspective, and the interactive process perspective; has been applied by the IS community to the analysis of software process improvement (SPI) innovations [11].

More recently, there have been some noteworthy attempts to provide a more holistic appreciation of the innovation landscape such as the compilations by Fagerberg [10] and by Shavinina [16]. However, Fagerberg's [6 p.20] conclusion that "our understanding of how knowledge-and-innovation operates at the organizational level remains fragmentary" and "that further conceptual and applied research is needed" indicates a scarcity of progress in the intervening period. Avgerou [2] comes to the striking conclusion that "the term innovation is not actually widely used" in the information systems literature. Swanson [17], who has been notable among the IS research community in addressing the subject, argues that the innovative deployment of information technology is "increasingly crucial to competitive survival and success."

The approach being taken in this research is to explore the use of Design Thinking in an innovation process – as a means of augmenting and enhancing the complete product life-cycle in Dell Inc.

A Multi-stakeholder Life-Cycle Perspective

"Designers' extraordinary sensitivity to what artifacts mean to others, users, bystanders, critics, if not for whole cultures, has always been an important but rarely explicitly acknowledged competence." [13, p. 48]

The statement above by Krippendorf emphasizes the importance of a multi-stakeholder perspective. Furthermore Krippendorff [13] goes on to state that "No artifact can be realized within a culture without being meaningful to those who can move it through its various definitions." Krippendorff 's emphasis on the lifecycle perspective suggests that designers should focus on the "before" the project, the "procurement" process of aligning actants in a design project and how the object of a design becomes this specific design object. Krippendorff's [13] perspective on ecology, influenced by Bateson [4], proposes that designers need to recognize the meaning of ecology of artifacts, stating that "Designers who can handle the ecological meaning of their proposals have a better chance of keeping their designs alive." People attach meaning to artifacts in relation to other artifacts. This relationship can span a number of dimensions e.g. cooperation, competition, interdependence, reproduction and retirement (death) of artifacts in specific contexts.

Krippendorff [13] emphasizes that designers need to seek a 2nd order understanding – i.e. employ design methods that allow them to gain some degree of understanding of the meaning different stakeholders ascribe to artifacts. Krippendorff suggests that designers increase their chances to design successful artifacts by taking into account four different perspectives on how individuals attribute meaning to artifacts: (i) The meaning of *artifacts in use*, (ii) the meaning of *artifacts in language*, (iii) the meaning of a *lifecycle of artifacts*, and (iv) the meaning of ecology *of artifacts*.

In the next section we will explore how Design Thinking is being implemented in Dell Inc. and, in particular, how a Multi-Stakeholder Life-Cycle Perspective is being advocated and executed in a real world environment.

3 Design Thinking in Dell Inc.

Customer/human-centred design can positively affect insight and idea generation in a natural and meaningful way by helping operations team members review chronic or open-ended problems with a new lens. Dell's experience has been consistent with other organizations that Design Thinking as a methodology can be applied to many problem spaces to come up with innovative solutions. Example problem domains which are described in this paper include:

1. Next Generation Enterprise Products : Cost reduction ideas generated both internally and with key suppliers,
   o Delivering next generation servers with better components and increased value, through smarter design and improved supply chain.
2. Service part delivery with a key Service Logistics partners: getting parts to customers more quickly,
   o Worked with stakeholders to identify pressure points in Dells service parts delivery chain, remove those hurdles, and so better meet Dell's Service Level Agreements (SLA's).
3. Software Procurement Software Request Tool: making it much easier to get business done with the organization
   o Used Design Thinking to generate a better business process to deliver software to Dell's internal business partners, thereby allowing them to meet Dells external customer's needs, more efficiently and effectively.
4. Dell Global Operations programmatic process for idea review (online portal for submission, seed review, director panel, exec review)

Dell's Global Operations organization excels in operational execution and is on transformative journey to become an even more innovative function. As part of that transformative journey, the organization reviewed various innovation tools. Design Thinking, as pioneered and practiced by the innovation consultancy IDEO, was decided upon as the desired tool to create innovative insights and ideas that would solve outstanding challenges for the function. Dell's learning in Design Thinking was initially informed directly by the IDEO method, and they adapted parts of the method to be more applicable to an operations-focused environment, including many deep dives on "extremes" within their operational data.

At a high level Design Thinking, like many other innovation methodologies, goes through several steps to frame, understand, and solve a problem. Those steps are:

a) **Define** the challenge in a human-centered way to inform the structure of the exercise

b) **Observe** and empathize with users of a particular process, tool, strategy, or product- whatever is related to the challenge that you are attempting to solve

c) **Form** insights based off of those user-centric observations that speak to users' needs, motivations, mental models, and desires

d) **Frame** opportunities informed by your insights. These are smaller and more actionable questions compared to the original challenge

e) **Brainstorm** solutions, going for a large volume of ideas that directly address user needs identified in earlier steps

f) **Prototype and experiment** rapidly to build out ideas and adjust solutions to improve them

Dell's Global Operations group has been able to apply the above framework to a variety of organizational challenges and create innovative solutions across a full ecosystem of partners, internal efforts, and our customers.

Examples of the Application of Design Thinking in Dell Inc.

3.1   Case #1: Cost Reductions in Dell Enterprise Products

Design Thinking Stage	Implementation in Case #1
Define the Challenge	In this case, ~~the~~ Dell's Head of Enterprise unit set an ambitious goal to reduce Cost of Goods Sold (CoGS) in Dells storage, networking, and server lines of business. The challenge was a very clear financial reduction target. A secondary challenge to overcome was that existing brainstorming practices had not been very collaborative, such that the outputs were not being implemented for lack of alignment across the relevant Lines of Business.
Observe and empathize	One of the key elements that was explored was reviewing the makeup of the brainstorming groupto ensure a cross-functional team, stressing the involvement ofboth senior leaders and morejunior team members to includea diversity of experience. It was decided there would be two different series of workshops, one with Dell internal stakeholders that would speak to internal questions Dell wanted to answer, the other would include some of Dell's key manufacturing partners in Asia to capture their viewpoints and insights into Dell's operations.
Form insights	All engaged in human-centered insights, but because this effort was coming from an operations organization, there was a much bigger emphasis on data collection, and including pareto analysis to understand where Dell's biggest opportunities lay. Key activities were interviews and data collection.

Frame opportunities / Brainstorm solutions	Scope of interviews: Internal teams (within global ops), but also outside the organisation. - One key learning discovered was that instead of getting desired cross-functional opinions, rather members would gravitate toward the same team members that they were somewhat familiar with in those organizations. To combat 'groupthink', Dell intentionally made the interview list include other stakeholders that would not typically engage. Dell also invited a subset of that team to brainstorm in the room. - Dell also interviewed suppliers and extended team members, who have visibility across the industry in terms of best practices. They also have the insights to understand what Dell does that may unintentionally add to their cost to serve Dell. - This innovation exercise would not be successful without customer insights. Therefore, members of the team also reached out to customers to better understand how they were using Dells existing products, what was the most useful, what was not in terms of features that were 'delighters'. After aligning participants on the pre-work that needed to be done - a workshop was planned. Day of the workshop: Beforehand, the team had created a social contract featuring aspirational rules like: - *"I understand that collaboration is key to our success"* - *"I understand that I am here to make a difference"*, And more tactical rules like: - *"I pledge to build on the ideas of others"*. - *"I pledge to have only one conversation at a time."* - *"Making things real"* : on the days of the brainstorming workshops, Dell ensured having actual products in the meeting room - though all of the team members contribute to the creation of the final product, being able to touch and take them apart, manipulate them, helps give a truer usability insight. - These insights were introduced by the workshop participants to the whole group, and were synthesized to identify more actionable opportunities that informed the brainstorming part of the workshop.

Prototype, experiment	**Outcomes:** Over two weeks of full day Design Thinking workshops, the team created a mass of over 2000 ideas, which were quickly amalgamated and pared down to a few hundred. The ideas have since been further vetted, built out into workplans, and are moving into implementation. The total value of the ideas generated there is in excess of $80M USD over the next three years and split across several major categories, namely: - Advanced sourcing opportunities and analytics into $-savings spend considerations. - Better supply chain management and enhanced use of existing supplier networks. - Collaborative sharing of cost reductions with Dells manufacturing partners. - Complexity reduction across Dell portfolio and $ spend activities. Getting the right mix of decision makers and diverse thinkers into the same room at the same time, and ensuring that all team members had generated insights prior to attending were the most crucial factors in the success of hitting the targets that the team was presented with. Ultimately, this reduced product manufacturing complexity , while delivering a much better value proposition to Dell's customers.

3.2   Case #2: Service Part Delivery with Latin America Service Delivery Partner

Design Thinking Stage	Implementation in Case #2
Define the challenge	Dell service logistics into Latin America, while very strong, still had growth opportunities, especially through the use of Dell's logistics partners. For Dell and its key logistics partner to work more effectively however, Dell Global Operations needed to conduct due diligence in a systematic fashion to understand precisely where they believed the opportunities existed and moreover, propose solutions to cement the partnership.
Observe and empathize	Service part delivery with Logistics Partner - getting service parts to customers more efficiently and effectively. Process: In an introductory meeting with key stakeholders, the team built out both process and extended stakeholder maps to determine who the "extreme users" were for this process. The stakeholders were then interviewed and observed to generate those observations. These included team members in both Dell headquarters as well as those heavily involved in the process across Latin America.

Form insights	Insight was also generated from feedback the team had received from end customers across Latin America.
	The core team assembled all of those stakeholders, created an interview and observation guide with which to engage these extreme users, and ultimately identified 5 key areas of opportunity: - Lead time reductions in delivery - Importer-of-record efficiency for customers in smaller Latin American countries - Multi-language invoices - Redistribution between Latin American countries
Frame opportunities and Brainstorm	- Lost products The team then brainstormed each opportunity space individually to generate ideas that could be executed internally and in concert with their partners. Those ideas are currently in
Prototype, experiment	implementation and are expected to affect several metrics: - Processing costs - Transportation costs - Inventory costs - Customer experience and NPS By engaging in a human-centered approach to understand where the "pain" was coming from in this logistics chain, the team was able to identify key fact-based opportunities for improvement in the supply chain. Moreover, they were able to brainstorm and are in the process of implementing ideas that will bring demonstrable value to customers by delivering products faster and cheaper than before, in conjunction with key partners.

3.3   Case #3: Software Procurement Request Tool

Design Thinking Stage	Implementation in Case #3
Define the challenge	The Software Procurement organization had set a goal of improving the tools and processes that they made available to their business partners within Dell. Primarily, the problem was that the existing process for business partners to request software was sometimes difficult to navigate, did not offer the optimum visibility into the procurement process, and sometimes required some duplicative reporting by the procurement commodity managers.

Observe and empathize	Software Procurement Software Request Tool - making it easier to get business done with the org, Goals: - The deliverable became an improved IT tool that would be simple for business partners to use, easy for SW mgmt. to manage workflows, and provide all parties with a single platform. Process: The team identified extreme users from which they would gather insights. That diverse group included: - Long time business partners - Newer business partners to the org - Veteran commodity managers - Transfer commodity managers from other organizations - Software procurement management
Form insights	Data analysis was conducted to identify which parts of the existing tool were actually being filled out by business partners, and which fields were being skipped over. The observation process included interviewing key users of the form, and also actually observing somebody using the tool for the very first time, such that the team could understand which parts were useful, which parts weren't, and which were confusing for any lay person.
Frame opportunities	Insights from those observations yielded several key opportunity spaces: - Business partners would regularly use only 25% of the fields available on the form, and more over most fields were not critical for commodity managers to execute their deals. - Software procurement regularly received many requests that should be actioned on by other Global Ops organizations - Commodity managers had to maintain separate note keeping systems and file to work around the existing intake tool
Brainstorm solutions	
Prototype, experiment	Brainstorming: The team brainstormed around each opportunity area, synthesized their ideas, and, using a wire-framing tool, rapidly prototyped to start getting solutions in the hands of executives and business partners alike as quickly as possible.

	That prototype, with changes along the way, is now serving a design spec for Dell team members in conjunction with outside partners to go and build out a "full-service" portal to meet the tacit and latent needs that were identified during the observation process.
	Used Design Thinking to generate a better business process to deliver software to our internal business partners, thereby allowing them to meet customer's needs out in the field better and faster.

4   Conclusions and Lessons Learned

In this paper we have examined three case studies of the application of Design Thinking in Dell Inc. in the context of current academic and practitioner thinking on Design Thinking. In particular, we think that the work resonates well with Kripendorf's [9] assertion that "Designers' extraordinary sensitivity to what artifacts mean to others, users, bystanders, critics, if not for whole cultures, has always been an important but rarely explicitly acknowledged competence." (8, p. 48). We see the practical application of how Design Thinking is being implemented in Dell Inc. and, in particular, how a Multi-Stakeholder Life-Cycle Perspective is being advocated and executed in a real world environment.

Practical lessons learned from this implementation of Design Thinking include:

(a) Understand and Capture User Needs from a Range of Diversified Stakeholders_
Though innovative methodologies and Design Thinking in particular, are often highlighted or exemplified by their application to consumer products, Dell has found that there can be a great amount of value created by using Design Thinking in a more operations-focused environment. The diversity of stakeholders needed to design, plan, manufacture, and deliver a product to a customer provides many opportunity to use this tool to very concretely define each user's needs and bake those into the processes and relationships that drive the business forward.

(b) Design Thinking Works Best in Symphony with Other Problem Solving
      Methodologies
Design Thinking is differentiated   because it stresses human-centered and user centered thinking, yet when applying it in an operations-focused environment, it is crucial that participants not discount other, more traditional inputs that we can use to derive insights while going through the discovery phase. From Dell's perspective, that means pulling together relevant value stream maps (or creating them where we observed gaps), existing strategy documents, and useful financial data. We found that these tools help create additional fact-based observations of the status quo for a given problem, and in the case of more visual tools, like value stream maps, that they helped teams truly examine "as-is" processes, compare those to stakeholders' existing mental models of how a given process worked, and then begin prototyping more effective need-based version of those processes.

(c) A more Refined Approach to Considering 'Ease of Implementation vs. Potential Value Creation '

Another key lesson learned concerns the post-brainstorm evaluation and approval mechanism for ideas within the organization. Often, teams will evaluate ideas and rank them relative to one another based on a simple matrix, where one axis is "potential value created" and the other is "ease of implementation" (Figure 1 below). One challenge is that this tended to discount the truly transformational ideas that came out of the exercise, so potentially valuable ideas that might take over 3 years to implement, or would require a major IT investment, were not getting visibility. One major adjustment that will be rolled out will be to encourage project teams to group ideas thematically and link them based on time to implementation. This will allow teams to seek approval for both ideas that are 'quick wins' and those that will take more time to mature and implement all at the same time, all the while providing a vision to Dell leadership as to what one can imagine an ideal state might look like for a given problem area.

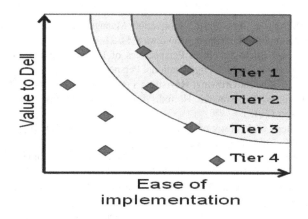

Fig. 1. Potential value created vs. Ease of Implementation

(d) Enhanced existing Hypothesis-testing approaches to problem solving

One of the reasons Design Thinking was chosen as a tool for Dell Global Operations is because it naturally complements the organization's existing reputation for excellence in execution. Much of Dell's competitive advantage has been derived from the organization's ability tocreation solutions based on hypothesis-driven problem solving and then quickly executing on those hypotheses. Design Thinking has furthered this approach by focusing on more exhaustive insight gathering upfront, forcing team members to intentionally make no assumptions about an answer until they have a very thorough understand of the entire problem, particularly from a human perspective.

5   Future Work

Efeoglu et al.'s [9] comprehensive review of the evolutions of Design Thinking methods indicates that Design Thinking methodologies are evolving and being adopted as mainstream activities embedded in innovation processes. This paper was reported on the application of Design Thinking in three projects in Dell Inc. where a Multi-Stakeholder Life-Cycle Perspective is being advocated and executed in a real world operations environment. Future research will explore how concepts such Design Thinking and Innovation impinge on each other as part of an initiative to improve Operational innovation processes. The research will explore how concepts such as Design Thinking might inform Innovation on Operations and also explore the impacts going the other direction – how can successful Operational Innovation processes inform and improve Design Thinking methods and tools in the future.

References

1. Adams, R., Besant, J., Phelps, R.: Innovation Management Measurement: A Review. International Journal of Management Reviews 8(1), 21–47 (2006)
2. Avgerou, C.: New Socio-Technical Perspectives of IS Innovation in Organizations. In: ICT Innovation: Economic and Organizational Perspectives (2002)
3. Bannon, L.J.: 20 Years a-Growing: Revisiting From Human Factors to Human Actors in Reframing Humans. In: Isomäki, H. (ed.) Information Systems Development, Samuli Pekkola, Springer (2011)
4. Bateson, G.: Steps to Ecology of Mind: Collected Essays in Anthropology, Psychiatry, Evolution, and Epistemology. University of Chicago Press (1972) ISBN 0-226-03905-6
5. Brown, T.: Change by design: How design thinking transforms organizations and inspires innovation. Harper Business, New York (2009)
6. Brown, T., Wyatt, J.: Design thinking for social innovation. Stanford Social Innovation Review 8(1), 30–35 (2010)
7. Cross, N.: Designerly Ways of Knowing: Design Discipline vs. Design Science. Design Issues 17(3), 49–55 (2001)
8. Dunne, D., Martin, R.: Design thinking and how it will change management education: An interview and discussion. Academy of Management Learning & Education 5(4), 512–523 (2006)
9. Efeoglu, A., Moller, A., Sérié, M., Boer, H.: Design thinking: characteristics and promises. In: Proceedings of 14th International CINet Conference on Business Development and Co-creation, Enschede, Continuous Innovation Network (CINet), pp. 241–256 (2013)
10. Fagerberg, J., Mowery, D., Nelson, R. (eds.): The Oxford Handbook of Innovation. Oxford University Press, Oxford (2005)
11. Kautz, K., Nielsen, P.A.: Understanding the Implementation of Software Process Improvement Innovations in Software Organizations. Information Systems Journal 14(1), 3–22 (2004)
12. Kelly, T.: The Art of Innovation: Lessons in Creativity from IDEO, America's Leading Design Firm. Doubleday, New York (2001)
13. Krippendorff, K.: The Semantic Turn: A New Foundation for Design. CRC Press (2006)
14. Plattner, H., Meinel, C., Weinberg, U.: design THiNK!NG – Innovation lernen, Ideenwelten öffnen. Mi-Wirtschaftsverlag, München (2009)

15. Slappendel, C.: Perspectives on Innovation in Organizations. Organization Studies 17(1), 107–129 (1996)
16. Shavinina, L. (ed.): The International Handbook on Innovation. Elsevier, Oxford (2003)
17. Swanson, E.: Information Systems Innovation among Organizations. Management Science 40(9), 1069–1088 (1994)
18. Verganti, R.: Design Driven Innovation: Changing the Rules of Competition by Radically Innovating What Things Mean. Harvard Business Press (2009)
19. Vetterli, C., Brenner, W., Uebernickel, F., Berger, K.: Dynamisches IT-Management: So steigern Sie die Agilität, Flexibilität und Innovationskraft Ihrer IT. Symposium Publishing, Düsseldorf (2012)
20. Wolfe, R.: Organizational Innovation: Review, Critique and Suggested Research Directions. Journal of Management Studies 31(3), 405–431 (1994)

Sustainable Connected Cities:
Vision and Blueprint towards Managing IT
for City Prosperity and Sustainability

Jim Kenneally[1], David Prendergast[1], Giovanni Maccani[2],
Brian Donnellan[2], and Markus Helfert[3]

[1] Intel Labs Europe, Intel Corporation, Leixlip, Co. Kildare, Ireland
{jim.kenneally,david.k.prendergast}@intel.com
[2] Innovation Value Institute, National University of Ireland Maynooth, Co. Kildare, Ireland
{giovanni.maccani.2013,brian.donnellan}@nuim.ie
[3] Business Informatics Group, Dublin City University, Dublin 9, Co. Dublin, Ireland
markus.helfert@computing.dcu.ie

Abstract. With the continued global trend of rural to urban population migration, traditional city management approaches are being challenged to both develop and sustainably manage the economies, societies and environments of
their cities. Many are turning to the application of computing technologies to
address these challenges. While computing technologies are becoming ever
more advanced, appropriate management approaches and frameworks for a city
to optimize contributions from such computing technologies are often lagging
behind. This paper presents a vision for sustainable connected cities (SCC), and
a nascent city management framework called the Sustainable Connected Cities
Capability Maturity Framework ^{TM} (SCC-CMF^{TM}) - for how to implement such
a vision, and a case study application. The contributions of design science research are briefly discussed in relation to these approaches.

Keywords: connected, cities, city, development, smart, intelligent, technology,
innovation, sustainable, sustainability, maturity, management.

1   Introduction

Today cities are estimated to be responsible for 80% of all global greenhouse gas
emissions [1], however they only account for approximately 50% of the global population [2]. Rural-to-urban migration is expected to reach over 70% of the world's
population living in cities by 2050 [1], escalating the upward pressures on the use of
available resources and environmental impacts – a trend recently highlighted by the
Fifth Assessment Report (AR5)[3] published by the Intergovernmental Panel on Climate Change (IPCC). Many of these challenges have consequences for cities to re-
think their governance regarding planning for long term development, competitive-
ness and sustainability. As a consequence, numerous city approaches are proposing a
portfolio of actions including the innovative employment of computing technologies
to stem or even reverse these urban pressures. Identifying relevant management

M. Helfert et al. (Eds.): EDSS 2013, CCIS 447, pp. 88–98, 2014.

artefacts can help make sense of these urban challenges and frame how cities can evolve sustainably by innovatively employing computing technologies.

2   Application of Design Science Research to Develop Artifacts

We selected Design Science Research (DSR), as it is a problem-driven approach to providing artifacts. DSR "creates and evaluates IT management artifacts intended to solve organizational problems" [4], P77. Table 1 presents an artifact typology of outputs from Design Science Research as defined by March and Smith [5]. Rossi and Sein [6], and Purao [7] propose a fifth artifact – listed as better theories, where DSR contributes to a better understanding of the phenomenon through reflection and abstraction. Table 1 displays the main artifact contributions of this paper.

Table 1. Design Science research Outputs

Output	Description	Main contributions of paper
Constructs	The conceptual vocabulary of a domain	Description of the Sustainable Connected Cities Capability Maturity Framework (SCC-CMF)
Models	A set of propositions or statements expressing relationships between constructs	Postulate on relationships amongst constructs
Methods	A set of steps used to perform a task – 'how to' knowledge	Cataloguing key activities postulated to assist maturity
Instantiations	The operationalization of constructs, models and methods	Case study application

Furthermore, Hevner et al.[4] offer guidelines for high-quality design research. Below describes the seven guidelines and how they are achieved within this paper:

1. Design as an Artefact: Design science research (DSR) involves a process to create artefact(s) - being any designed object with an embedded solution to an understood research problem [8]. Table 1 illustrates the resultant artefacts from this paper's research.
2. Problem Relevance: The objective of design-science research is to develop technology-based solutions to important and relevant business problems [4]. Section #1 and #3 outline the Relevance Cycle with-regard-to specifying the domain problem, opportunity and potential.
3. Design Evaluation: The utility, quality, and efficacy of a design artefact must be rigorously demonstrated via well-executed evaluation methods [4]. The Sustainable Connected Cities Capability Maturity Framework (SCC-CMF) is evaluated using a combination of descriptive evaluation method (using informed argument and scenarios with information from the knowledge base and the opinions of experts); and then moving to observational evaluation (using a case study approach). Artefacts were

evaluated in terms of correctness, completeness and utility of the constructed artefacts.

4. Research Contributions: Effective design-science research must provide clear and verifiable contributions in the areas of the design artefact, design foundations, and/or design methodologies [4]. This paper describes how the three cycles of design science research (DSR) activities [9] can be applied to an emerging research domain of Smart Cities. The paper also contributes to defining the acceptance criteria for evaluation of resultant design artifacts for Smart Cities by applying past knowledge to building novel design science artefacts for the Rigor Cycle.

5. Research Rigor: DSR relies upon the application of rigorous methods in both the construction and evaluation of the design artefact [4]. Sections #4-6 of this paper outline the Rigor Cycle, applying past knowledge to building novel design science artefacts.

6. Design as a Search Process: The research should be organized as a search for the solution of the problem [4]. Sections #7-8 outline the Design Cycle regarding iterating between building and evaluating the artifacts.

7. Communications of Research: DSR must be presented effectively both to science-oriented as well as practice-oriented audiences [4]. The publication of this paper in proceedings of EDSS serves to address both academic and practitioner audiences, given the general cross-sectional appeal of EDSS audiences.

The remainder of this paper broadly aligns to the three cycles of DSR activities defined by Hevner [9] and Takeda et al. [10] five stage iterative approach:

1. Problem awareness: Section #1 and #3 - identifies what the problem is and why it is a problem.

2. Suggestion: Section #4 suggests the solution to the identified problem – i.e. the Sustainable Connected Cities Capability Maturity Framework ^{TM} (SCC-CMF^{TM})

3. Development: Sections #5-7 develops the solution (i.e. artefacts).

4. Evaluation: Section #8 tests and validates the artifacts by presenting a case study application of these artefacts.

5. Conclusion: Section #9 offers summary and general conclusions.

3   Underpinning Knowledge Base

Traditional approaches associated with organizational management theory begin to break-down, or at their very best – border on being over-stretched, when applied to managing something as complex as a city. However, approaching the management of cities in terms of the resources a city possesses and the organizational capabilities required to manage those resources may hold potential for how to manage IT for city prosperity and sustainability.

Much of the published literature in this space can be related to the resource-based view (RBV) for examining the competitive advantage of a firm, stating such advantages lay primarily in the application of a bundle of valuable tangible or intangible resources at the firm's disposal - resources that are neither perfectly imitable nor substitutable without great effort [11]. However, RBV does not sufficiently illuminate what are the management mechanisms associated with these specific resources and how they may help the firm achieve superior performance. Dynamic capability view (DCV) aims to fill this through the clarification of management mechanisms that are required to integrate and reconfigure resources by focusing attention on the firm's ability to renew its resources in line with changes in its environment.

The authors postulate that the RBV and DCV can offer new perspectives on how to approach management of IT for city sustainability and prosperity. Dynamic capabilities are defined as "the firm's ability to integrate, build, and reconfigure internal and external competences to address rapidly changing environments" [12]. Obviously, the concept of a city may be different from that of a firm; however the city can be considered as a collection of resources, requiring appropriate mechanisms to confer superior city performance from its resources – similar to that of a firm.

4   Introducing Sustainable Connected Cities Capability Maturity Framework ^{TM} (SCC-CMF^{TM})

To provide a systematic means to frame, evaluate and manage the sustainable development of cities and to help guide decisions about people, policy, infrastructure, investment, and the use of computing technologies; Intel Labs Europe, the Innovation Value Institute at NUI Maynooth, and the Business Informatics Group at Dublin City University, in collaboration with Dublin City Council, have researched the *Sustainable Connected Cities Capability Maturity Framework^{TM} (SCC-CMF^{TM})*.

The SCC-CMF aims to

- Unwrap the complex ecosystem of a city into domains for tackling city sustainability
- Provide a common language between diverse stakeholders to set goals, evaluate improvements and benchmark over time
- Offer scenarios that are vendor independent and technology implementation neutral
- Define improvement roadmaps using milestones and reference landmarks

A capability based view (CBV) framework is designed to provide a stable view of the entity under investigation. While a city's municipalities, management hierarchies, processes, technologies or people might reorganize, a capability is more enduring and constant. Capabilities possess properties such as the people, processes, and technologies that are used to instantiate the capability. They can be hierarchical; containing nested relationships, as well as horizontal connections.

The SCC-CMF taxonomy comprises of six city domains (A) - refer to Figure 1 - for tackling city sustainability, each domain is managed by the use of an enabling platform (B) to drive sustainability and connectedness within and across the six domains, for impact across a city's economy, environment and society (C).

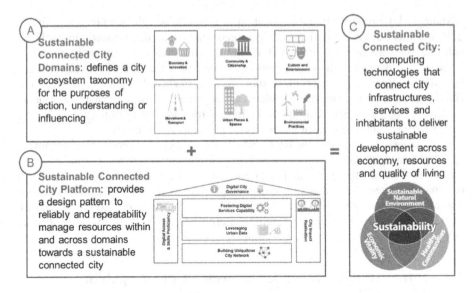

Fig. 1. Sustainable Connected Cities Capability Maturity Framework Overview

The SCC-CMF's objective is to present a 'whole systems perspective' towards achieving sustainable cities, enabling joined up thinking and co-ordination on key issues across interests groups such as city inhabitants, municipalities, businesses, local/national legislation, policy makers, etc. It can offer a city-wide guiding structure to co-ordinate and provide direction towards the achievement of sustainable city outcomes.

5   Sustainable Connected City Domains

The domains of SCC-CMF are generically defined as an:

> City ecosystem classification, according to their homogeneity for the purposes of action, understanding or influencing advancement towards a sustainable connected city.

More specifically, they are designed to represent a city taxonomy; namely

- Economy & Innovation: facilitating human capital[1] towards knowledge economy, commerce vitality, entrepreneurship, employment, and flexibility.
- Community & Citizenship: improving social capital[2] towards individual and community well-being, participation, inclusion, health and safety.
- Culture & Entertainment: promoting cultural heritage, involvement and accessibility.

---

[1] Human capital: How people's skills and knowledge can contribute to economic and social value.

[2] Social capital: How the attitude, spirit and willingness of people to network, engage, and co-operate with each other in achieving collective activities such as community improvement and civic engagement. In this way social capital represents the value and power of the social bonds and social networks created between individuals and their communities.

- Movement & Transport: managing transport systems and services for accessible and sustainable travel behaviour choices.
- Urban Places & Spaces: managing vitality and viability of open spaces, residential and commercial buildings towards a coherent urban structure.
- Environmental Practices: managing environmental and biodiversity impact.

Applying a combination of design science research and grounded theory method [14], these domains describe a broad range of characteristics associated with Sustainable Connected Cities (SCC) – Figure 2 - where computing technologies intelligently connect a city for the sustainable development of its economy, environment and quality of living.

Fig. 2. Sustainable Connected Cities Domains and Objectives

A rigorous review of academic publications and international city trends informed the definition of SCC Domains and the characteristics within them, including consulting Dublin City's Development Plan [15] and Giffinger et al [16]. However, SCC Domains are adaptable for adding to and subtracting from; based on individual city context and circumstances. A full examination pertaining to the development of these domains is beyond the scope of this paper, refer to Maccani et al [17] which covers this topic in more detail.

6   Sustainable Connected City Enabling Platform

To achieve sustainable connected city outcomes within and across each of these six domains, the SCC Enabling Platform provides a design pattern[3] - Figure 3 - to

---

[3] Design pattern is generally reusable template solution to commonly re-occurring challenges.

Manage key resources (both tangible and intangible) towards achieving sustainable connected city outcomes.

This design pattern can be used within a single domain and across all domains, for an entire city or within a single city neighborhood or city project. The remainder of this section outlines the philosophies, together with examples, for each element of the enabling platform.

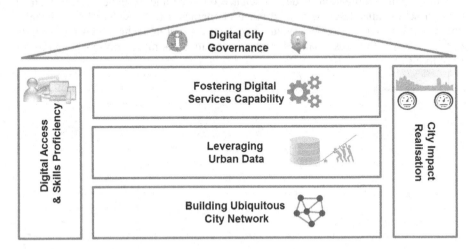

Fig. 3. Sustainable Connected Cities Enabling Platform

- Digital City Governance: Promoting unified governance to how resources are applied across city departments and municipalities can be a key enabler for management towards sustainable connected cities.

- Digital Access & Skills Proficiency: To advance human and social capital to leverage the IT revolution requires promoting digital inclusion and savviness for both city dwellers and city employees.

- Building Ubiquitous City Network: Underlying this concept are the fundamentals of instrumentation (e.g. sensors) and interconnectedness (many networked devices integrated to a city network or network of networks) to provide the necessary city network infrastructure.

- Leveraging Urban Data: promotion of open standards for data management across city departments is the catalyzing platform for city-wide integration and leveraging of urban data.

- Fostering Digital Service Capabilities: new capabilities are needed across all levels, to envision and transform city services by applying information technologies in more innovative ways.

- City Impact Realization: moving towards triple bottom line accounting expands traditional reporting by acknowledging, in addition to the economic performance, also the ecological and social impact when measuring success.

The Sustainable Connected City Enabling Platform can be applicable at any level of managing a sustainable connected city hierarchy; from city-wide, to subset of city districts, a single community, to delivery teams or at individual project level.

7 SCC-CMF Dynamic Feedback Loop

SCC-CMF is architected as a dynamic feedback loop, i.e. by applying SCC-CMF, maturity can be calibrated, appropriate actions selected and executed. Maturity can be recalibrated by running the feedback loop once more, every loop stimulating new maturity actions that move closer to overall SCC goals. These feedback loops can run in macro and micro cycles amongst all elements of the framework[4]. Figure 4 illustrates the feedback loop, plus identification of nascent key activities associated with driving maturity within each of the enabling platform elements.

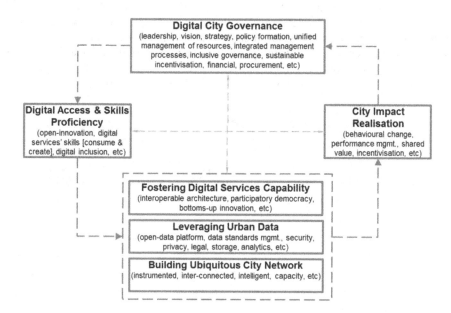

Fig. 4. Sustainable Connected Cities Enabling Platform – Feedback Loop

The intent is to incrementally evolve a city, where computing technologies intelligently connect a city for the sustainable development of its economy, environment and quality of living. Maccani et al [13] summarize key published literature on the impact from employing computing technologies towards better city management of its economy, environment, and society, including improved outcomes across traffic, education, health and well-being, employment, entrepreneurship, e-government, waste management, public safety, food, water and energy supply.

---

[4] SCC-CMF architecture leverages the Innovation Value Institute's IT Capability Maturity Framework (IT-CMF). The research team would like to thank Martin Curley (originator of IT-CMF) for suggestions in blueprinting SCC-CMF.

8   Dublin City Case Study: Application of SCC-CMF

Dublin City was seeking a management artifact that would help shape the city's digital future and provide a guide for the city to leverage new technologies that will enhance the city's economic vitality, social well-being and environmental balance. The development of SCC-CMF involved intense collaboration from Dublin City officials. This collaboration used a combination of means when developing SCC-CMF, including expert (or face) validity[5], construct validity[6], and empirical validity[7]. Regarding expert and construct validities, a great deal of attention was given to ensuring the various artifacts were clear, easy to comprehend and that all the relevant factors were comprehended. This involved leveraging relevant academic and international practitioner approaches, together with informed and reasoned discussions to develop the design science artifacts outlined in Table 1 and expanded upon in subsequent sections of this paper.

To test empirical validity, a city workshop involving city stakeholder representatives including municipalities, service providers, business groups, transport bodies, environmental agencies, community organizations, councils, etc, and city dwellers to assess the current level of Dublin's SCC maturity and to define how Dublin city can improve its maturity for city sustainability. A maturity scoring rubric was employed to evaluate Dublin City on the SCC Enabling Platform within each of the six SCC domains.

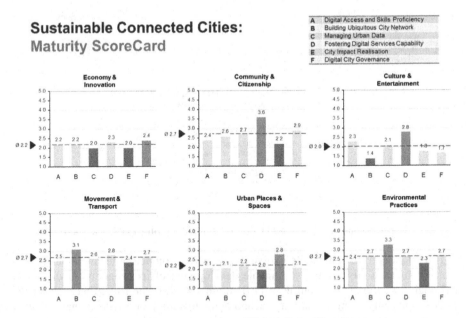

Fig. 5. Summary Result from SCC Maturity Workshop

---

[5] Face validity is often used to assess whether artifacts appear to make sense.
[6] Construct validity relates to whether all the relevant factors are captured and whether all the appropriate relationships between those factors have been identified and incorporated.
[7] Empirical validity is used to assess, describe, and recognize causal patterns at work through empirical analyses.

Figure 5 summarizes quantitative data collected across the six SCC domains. Leading maturity domain are 'Movement & Transport', 'Community & Citizenship' & 'Environmental Practices', while lagging domains are 'Culture & Entertainment'.

As well as quantitative data collected, arrays of qualitative information were solicited using expert facilitators and the SCC-CMF to guide dialogue. The qualitative and quantitative insights from the workshop provided the foundation for creating Dublin's first Digital MasterPlan, unveiled by EU Commissioner Neelie Kroes and Dublin's Lord Mayor in June 2013 - this Digital MasterPlan defines a roadmap for making Dublin a dynamic and technology enabled city [18].

9   Conclusion

The challenge for cities will be to redefine the city as a platform for innovation to shape its own sustainable future leveraging innovative computing technologies. What is required is a form of city-wide swarm intelligence where the collective behavior of a city's decentralized nature can be coordinated according to universal principles and consistent approaches. This paper outlines the nascent potential of the Sustainable Connected City Capability Maturity Framework to enhance a city's capacity to identify more meaningful approaches towards effectively leveraging computing technologies across its city ecosystem for sustainable outcomes.

Further research is underway on extending the SCC-CMF including, growing international city case studies, researching best practices within the SCC Enabling Platform, cataloguing of world-wide city projects in each SCC domain, defining key-performance-indicators (KPIs) for benchmarking across cities, and expanding SCC maturity assessment instruments outside a workshop delivery.

Acknowledgements. The authors would like to thank Dublin City Council for their expert contributions, discussions and case study application when constructing and refining this research. This research is funded by Intel Corporation and the Irish Research Council (IRC).

Disclaimer. The opinions expressed are those of the authors and may not reflect official positions of their affiliated organizations.

References

1. World Bank, Cities and Climate Change: An Urgent Agenda (2010), http://go.worldbank.org/26YQJJJPWO (last accessed June 23, 2013)
2. The United Nations, UNFPA State of World Population, Report, The United Nations Population Fund (EN-SWOP2011-FINAL.pdf) (2011), http://foweb.unfpa.org/SWP2011/reports/
3. Intergovernmental Panel on Climate Change (IPCC), Fifth Assessment Report (AR5), http://www.ipcc.ch/ (last accessed September 30, 2013)
4. Hevner, S., March, J., Park, S.: Design Science Research in Information Systems. Management Information Systems Quarterly 28(1), 75–105 (2004)

5. March, S.T., Smith, G.F.: Design and natural science research on information technology. Decision Support Systems 15, 251–266 (1995)
6. Rossi, M., Sein, M.: Design Research Workshop: A Proactive Research Approach. Presentation delivered at IRIS 26, August 9 – 12 (2003)
7. Purao, S.: Design Research in the Technology of Information Systems: Truth or Dare. GSU Department of CIS Working Paper. Atlanta (2002)
8. Peffers, K., Tuunanen, T., Rothenberger, M.A., Chatterjee, S.: A Design Science Research Methodology for Information Systems Research. Journal of Management Information Systems 24(3), 45–47 (2008)
9. Hevner, A.: The three cycle view of design science research. Scandinavian Journal of Information Systems 19(2), 87 (2007)
10. Takeda, H., Veerkamp, P., Tomiyama, T., Yoshikawa, H.: Modeling Design Processes. American Association for Artificial Intelligence AI Magazine 11(4), 37–48 (1990)
11. Barney, J.B.: Firm Resources and Sustained Competitive Advantage. Journal of Management 17(1), 99–120 (1991)
12. Teece, D., Pisano, G., Shuen, A.: Dynamic Capabilities and Strategic Management. Strategic Management Journal 18(7), 509–533 (1997)
13. Maccani, G., Donnellan, B., Helfert, M.: A Comprehensive Framework for Smart Cities. In: SMARTGREENS 2013 Conference, Aachen (May 2013)
14. Gregory, R.: Design Science Research and the Grounded Theory Method: Characteristics, Differences, and Complementary Uses. In: ECIS 2010 Proceedings. Paper 44 (2010)
15. Dublin City, Development Plan 2011-2017 – Volume 1: Written Statement, Dublin City Council Publication (2010), http://www.dublincitydevelopmentplan.ie/downloads2.php (last accessed August 9, 2013)
16. Giffinger, R., Fertcher, C., Kramar, H., Kalasek, R., Meijers, E.: Smart Cities – Ranking of European Medium-size Cities. Vienna University of Technology (October 2007)
17. Maccani, G., Donnellan, B., Helfert, M., Kenneally, J., Prendergast, D.: Applying Grounded Theory to Explore Smart City Services within an Action Design Research Project, working paper
18. Dublin City Council, A Digital Masterplan for Dublin, Shaping Our Digital Future (2013), http://digitaldublin.ie/masterplan/ (last accessed August 30, 2013)

Solution Prototyping with Design Thinking – Social Media for SAP Store: A Case Study

Arkın Efeoğlu[1,2], Charles Møller[2], and Michel Sérié[1]

[1] SAP Deutschland AG & Co.KG, Service Innovation, Walldorf, Germany
[2] Center for Industrial Production, Aalborg University, Aalborg, Denmark
arkin.efeoglu@sap.com

Abstract. Information and knowledge workers as well as other employees who are not part of a research or product development team are barely exposed to innovation creation processes. Design Thinking as an innovation method is typically used in R&D. This research analyses whether a short-cycled Design Thinking method can be developed, so employees outside R&D can be taken out of their daily jobs and innovate without falling too much behind with their operational work. Alongside with short-cycled DT session there are potential impacts on business and hence on management. Business Thinking barriers are tried to be broken and Design Thinking advantages are increasingly preferred by management. This case study based paper provides key insights into how DT phases and behavior can be changed for creating synergy across employees, management and products from which the end-consumer benefits. The Social Media for SAP store case study combines a conceptual and product oriented solution derivation with Design Thinking.

Keywords: Solution Prototype, short-cycled Design Thinking, Prototyping, Social Media, Enterprise 2.0.

1 Theoretical Background and Relevance

The interaction with Enterprise Information Systems (EIS) is changing. Simplicity and social-interaction demands are changing also the game for business software. Business software needs to keep pace with consumer oriented hardware and software trends. Flexibility of architecture and robustness of software is no longer sufficient. Present business school students, respectively tomorrow's top managers and decision makers demand a different way of interaction with business software [1]. The SAP store's objective is to provide an environment where business software can be purchased and easily consumed, that is highly interactive and social. Multi-sensory devices and software for instance the development of more accurate and conversational voice recognition (i.e.: SIRI from Apple Computer), or technologically advanced glasses with on-view information (i.e.: Google Glass) and instant connectivity to peers, colleagues and experts change employees interaction with business systems.

M. Helfert et al. (Eds.): EDSS 2013, CCIS 447, pp. 99–110, 2014.

2   Research Objective

Classic Design Thinking particularly fit to research and development teams and are pretty much product or service-oriented only. The objective of researching this case study is to gain insights on how Design Thinking is being used in organizations outside research and product development teams. The objective is to find a DT method that goes in harmony and accommodates with participants' daily work. The study is more interested in conducting Design Thinking in accelerated or adopted way for all employees in an organization. Especially for those who spend most of their working time on operational tasks are being measured on their operational or quarter-based results. The hypothesis is that the design thinking methodology needs to be slightly tweaked to fit employees and managers who are rather occasionally and especially temporarily exposed to DT. Such short-cycled Design Thinking Workshops have also the characteristics of forming new corporate programs or projects and serve as kickoff. Another type of short-cycled DT projects seems to be rather suitable for conceptual design challenges.

Nevertheless, the contributions to the innovativeness of occasional DT practioners are not less than employees who are constantly exposed to DT. This is the reason why the lead author calls this type of DT workshop with duration of maximum one week, short-cycled DT.

Hypothesis 1: *Short-cycled Design Thinking sessions require an adaption to the DT method.*

Hypothesis 2: *Usages of short-cycled DT sessions have a more positive and constructive impact on business than typical business thinking oriented management.*

This explorative and analytical case study may serve first to recognize and understand the DT phases and its elements that can be adjusted. With the feedback of managers, the participants possible dedication during and shortly after the sessions the impact of DT on the overall business and the management's assessment on DT value will be analyzed alongside.

Hypothesis 3: *Distinguishing factor of short-cycled DT is the earliest possible prototyping.*

Method wise, the hypothesis is that the most coining solution to the design challenge is gained with the first run of all phases from problem space to solution space. The first run-through shapes the rough solution direction and fixes the mind of the participants.

The lead author emphasizes on the distinction between the two types of short-cycled DT methods used. One that is used for product-centric design challenges and the others on strategic or conceptual design thinking challenges. As this case study will demonstrate there can be overlaps between the two.

The learnings and key insights will be taken over to the future action-research oriented conduction of future short-cycled DT sessions.

3   Method

The Design Thinking Approach Applied on the Case Study
A sequential representation of Design Thinking is used for the case study. Particularly SAP Design Thinking approach is applied. SAP's DT Method is fully compliant with Stanford approach that merely uses a different naming of phases. The difference between both is the additional step of "implementation" in the SAP method [31]. Newell et al. (1967) mentioned the problem space back in 1967, and asked for a comprehensive understanding of the problem, believing that a solution can be derived directly from within the inner structure of the problem. Forty years later, Cross and Dorst (2007) defined the "co-evolution of problem and solution", i.e. the exploration of both the problem and the solution space in parallel [8]. Both SAP and Stanford DT approaches follow Cross' suggestion of problem and solution space separation. A direct relation between problem and solution space is given at any time through the iteration capabilities from an arbitrary DT step to the other, irrespective of project state.

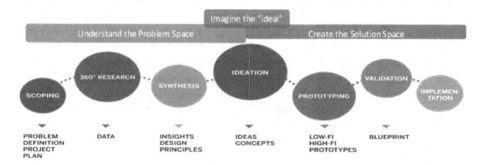

Fig. 1. Imagine, Create & Innovate - Design Thinking with SAP [31]

3.1   The Prototypes as Core Element of Design Thinking

The prototype as the central DT element or artifact is supposed to serve as a prescriptive means to solve the design challenge in the design challenge. According to March and Smith (2010) the "conceptualizations are extremely important in both natural and design science. They define the terms used when describing and thinking about tasks". Models are situated between the problem space and solution space helping to explore the effects of design decisions and the impact of changes in the real world [3]. Models use constructs to depict a real world situation, hence the design problem and solution space [33]. In Design Thinking a model for a conceptual design challenge would also represent a prototype. This is implied by the fact that design thinking not only serves for product innovation but also for service or solution innovation. Failing IT projects have their roots in underestimating the complexity and its fit for purpose. Thus there is a particular importance on the prototype as an instantiation with its problem solving characteristics. The instantiation demonstrates the feasibility and its suitability in a real world environment [16].

In the general IS literature, evaluation is generally regarded from one of two perspectives. In the ex-ante perspective, candidate systems or technologies are evaluated before they are chosen and acquired or implemented. In the ex-post perspective, a chosen system or technology is evaluated after it is acquired or implemented [20]. The prototype as a potential predecessor or conceptual excerpt of a final product will focus on the ex-ante perspective.

4   The SAP Store DT Case Study

At the center of the study is particularly the prototyping and the possibility to adjust other phases for an optimized short-cycled Design Thinking. In order to determine adjustable phases, the findings per DT phase are analyzed separately but also analyzed in the context of the full cycle. In addition to the DT phases/ steps the characteristics like heterogeneity of team members and DT typical rules of engagement. Starting with the team setup, there has been two teams formed for this purpose. The names of the participants are anonymized, but their positions are as is:

Every Design Thinking Workshop is based on the DT approach by the d.school (Stanford) or SAP method and hence requires a Design Challenge to kick-off the Workshop. For this workshop the design challenge is: *How can we use social media to support enterprise buyers in finding, evaluating and buying SAP solutions at the SAP Store?*

The Design Challenge has been co-defined with the DT coaches and the client. The clients in this case are two responsibles from the SAP store lead team. The formulation of the Design Challenge should neither limit topic wise the scope of the Workshop nor overarch unnecessary parts. The terms were selected carefully such as "...finding, evaluating and buying..."

Solution Space

Prototyping
At the core of this research is the prototyping phase, the behavior and the potential impact on the business. Nevertheless, if the previous phases aren't done properly or poorly the result of the prototype is also poor as the decision and idea base is limited. After the ideation phase the two teams agree to share the prototype's development and build only one with complementary elements. One team is taking over the conceptual part considering the entire social and technical system of trying and buying software. The other team focuses into the details of the SAP store as well as the SAP solutions with social networking capabilities.

The team with the responsibility to develop the concept thinks about wider impact onto SAP's business. They try to find the right mix of tasks that should be part of SAP and be mentored and those parts of the business that should be autonomous to the community. The degree of SAP involvement for social network related decision making is being defined. The participants agree that the social media for SAP Store is about SAP business software only (not partner solution or alike) and the platform is not used by SAP to make marketing directly.

The prototype helps to build the business case for the management to whom the results and idea is proposed. The persona defined helps the team to focus on the purpose of the prototype and not distract. For the social media and social network part of the

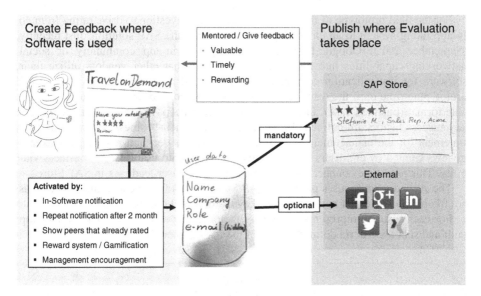

Fig. 2. The social media for SAP store interaction concept

design challenge, the team recognizes and spends considerable high amount of time to find a working model for an intrinsically motivated reward system that makes the end-users contribute very positively. The team uncovered the potential of a feedback loop directly from the end-users, where the idea is to directly give the feedback to the SAP developer or development organization. Currently product development receives feedback via own sales people, written format or typically indirectly.

The team also empathizes with other roles involved in the process of a "socialized SAP store", particularly with SAP sales people who would not always want the full transparency of feedback given by frustrated end-users. The concern is on the danger of publicly available uncontrolled and uncensored feedback. The threat that is recognized here is also seen as a big chance and opportunity to dramatically improve enterprise systems. (Positive) Peer rating is seen more important than any other software feature or rewarding etc. Because this type of positive rating can help scale the software purchase and acquisition through the SAP store much faster than any other sales channel. The rating for enterprise systems can be blessing and a curse. In case, an end-user wants to rate negatively there will be external rating platforms with the freedom the user has that can be used. It seems that providing this environment by the software vendor is considered better than leaving it to uncontrolled areas. The self-moderation option of a SAP-owned social media platform for business systems allows that users help each other reducing ultimately the support effort of the business systems vendor. The teams also made use of behaviors from non-software industries to assess a potential success of a social network platform by a software vendor. The example is around car manufacturers. If car owners have questions around their cars, they least likely use the car vendor websites but rather search for independent automobile communities. The uncertainty of the success of software vendor moderated social platform remains.

For the final prototype of the concept there is the suggestion to drive rating from an In-app rating system to an embedded community into the SAP solution. Just recently (September 2013) Google launched these type of in-app community or social networking capabilities into their browser, showing that other vendors utilize their software for in-application community embedding. It takes around 2/3 of the total prototyping time until the team starts to structure the concept into a business present-able format (business case). In the later stages the concept is further detailed out and key success factors are defined. Team one concludes their business case with the key statement for the management as follows: For business decision makers, ratings and reviews created by end-users provide holistic insights into usability and business via-bility. This prototype connect software evaluation with user feedback in SAP Store.

The second team focuses purely on SAP Store and its future capabilities. The ideas are filtered and assessed mainly by their key features and hence success factors.

For each visually representable success factor, there was a user interface mockup built and success criteria defined as part of the management presentation.

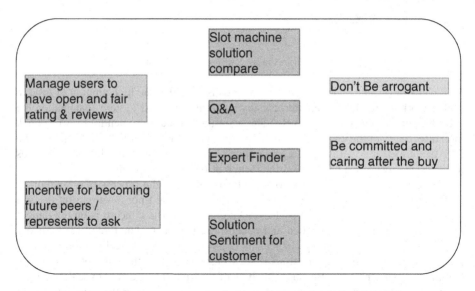

Fig. 3. The four success categories (red boxes) for the "socialized" SAP Store

The second team discusses details of the solution comparison. From the analogy of web shops with consumer product comparison, the team agrees on a mandatory first selection of a business system that is taken as a benchmark or comparison basis. The teams start with paper mockups and wireframes. In some instances where there is two alternatives the team members just voted democratically on which one to continue on. This avoids long during discussions. Voting had the advantage of not justifying one artifact (=solution segment or mockup alternative) over another. Every team member is able to individually explain the prototype, every single element and ready to defend challenging questions. Open questions, details of functionalities or processual ques-tions are partially solved by simulation of instances. A role play for instance of an end-user is simulated. For instance, solving the expert's question, the team try to clarify who and how many experts can be involved and who should be giving the answer. The role play simulated the end user's question: "I am running Linux, will this solution run with my operating system version?". With similar other open questions the team is aware of the level of the required solution and accordingly not bothering with very detailed open points. The expert discussion leads to further discussion that cannot be resolved being too much focused on the naming "expert". Calling it differently helps the participants to accept as compromise. For the particular situation the term "consulting" was better accepted than the "expert". The team understands that the future users want more visual elements. Visual and icons can be recognized quicker than text-centric enterprise systems.

Findings from the Prototyping Phase

• Problem Space helps to see the challenge in its broader context ultimately not only defining a solution for the particular challenge but also considering an entire concept and system (natural evolvement of developing something like system dynamics)

• Let go with the dynamics of the workshop. Don't be to dogmatic on the approach. Allow for detours, rule breaking in terms of doing things different than the method allows. In this case this is the job (prototype) sharing

• Further questions arise the more tangible the prototypes become. These questions lead to iterating back to problem space and further clarification. Without prototyping which is a kind of a rehearsal, many things aren't thought through

• Team coherence is maximum enforced through prototyping.

• Prototyping is latest point in time where disagreement, misalignment and different perspectives are harmonized for the sake of the project success

• The created prototype is a manifestation of theories infusing soul to a project

• Drawing the persona next to the concept solution proposal helps staying focused on the challenge

• Heterogeneous and open minded people don't see risks only negative, but also as a positive chance to change into the right direction (i.e.: publicly feedback transparency)

• For truly active team members the temporary unavailability of team members, who need to join other meetings is easily coverable

• Whiteboard is a key prototyping tool. The easy changeability in contrary to fixed notes is a very big advantage of reshuffling thoughts

• Prototyping phase is recognized as more important phase than ideation, many new ideas, more realistic and implementable ideas are created during the prototyping

• After the first iteration of prototyping the iteration between prototyping and ideation is happening seamlessly. The first biggest idea manifests quickly and is rather immobile in terms of idea change, especially when prototyping starts. The probability that a low-fidelity prototype is quickly dismissed is rather unlikely

• Procedural details are visually thought through with the persona (what would the persona "do next") implying to develop successively the prototype/ concept

• Prototyping is excluded from diverging and converging. This is an emotional, highly team-dynamic exercise.

• The involvement of the client/ product owner (in scrum terms) in the team during prototyping doesn't influence the prototype negatively as the client gets into the team flow/ mood

• The highest empathy level of the persona is developed with the prototype as the persona is always the center of reference

• Picking the most important ideas from plenty of ideas (filtering) is difficult because the team members are emotionally attached to their own ideas, not wanting them to loose.

• Business case or management presentation is better off with visually depicted prototypes that can be grasped fast along with the textual success criteria that need is made aware

• Risks or open points must also be addressed in the business case/ mgmt. presentation

• Analogies (industries, products, life situations) help understanding the problem and ideas better. At least analogies serve as a foundation

• Internal voting for decision making in a team can save time and avoid decision justifications and discussions

• Although prototyping is a kind of a sticky notes free zone, there is a very good usage for the quick sequencing of the user interaction (process description). From post-it sequences to paper mockups to wireframes to low-fidelity digital mockups

• Role play and mental run-throughs are key for further elaboration and detailing prototypes

• The objective principal or the subject matter expert can kindly influence the group to re-focus on expected direction

• Terminologies can set expectations leading to long-taking discussions. Use of certain terminology like the "expert" sets expectations in the mind of the participants causing further discussion of acceptance of the role. By replacing the term "expert" with "consultant" the participants changed their perspective and broadened the acceptance on engagement role

• Many participants think in analogies and competitive solutions that only can lead to incremental improvements or continuous innovation but not into breakthrough innovation. For a enterprise systems vendor this might be acceptable but more difficult in other industries. Concrete example is the "log-in tunneling. Login into SCN with Facebook account or example of live tiles from Microsoft"

• Towards the end of the prototype, among the participants there is a relief mode noticeable due to the team's achievement

• Business related DT with employees do not distract with other topics. The participants are constantly focused on solving the challenge particularly the prototype. The result orientation and delivery attitude seems not to have room for mental breaks. It feels like participants are "working" while enjoying to have fun.

Holistic Insights and Conclusion of the Full Design Thinking Cycle

- In all phases the participants educate each other and learn more details about the subject of the design challenge (i.e.: what can enterprise systems vendors benefit from participation of their user in twitter; how can sentiment analysis be leveraged)
- The capability that a non-expert from this area could present the entire story impresses management and gives trust into the project
- Executive Vice President and project sponsor says that he "...increasingly sees the distinguishing value of Design Thinking led projects and that..." he is "...amazed by the results"
- Early prototyping is at the core of every DT engagement, irrespective of duration and purpose (design challenge type)
- Job sharing and team assignment to elements of the entire solution might make sense.
- The better the team comprehension about the problem, the more aligned the team members are for the presented results. The intrinsic motivation and the identification with the solution is significantly high. Knowledge about the details of the solution and why something has been decided a certain way is equally distributed
- Provisioning of information to the team, transparency and availability of information and trust on data source is key for research and entire problem space
- Spending considerable time on building and scheduling the agenda is a major advantage - Organization of speakers, companies and interview partners is very important and changes the quality of the outcome and opens up for objective perspectives on the topic (improves out of the box thinking)
- The definition of the design challenge may limit the scope of possible solutions
- The prototyping of the concept as well as the future determination of Social Media and the SAP store with its entire systemized environment makes the solution prototype
- An additional harmonization session for all teams is valuable, if all teams are given the same design challenge (end of synthesis and end-of evaluation as a kind of super-prototype)
- Ones a full cycle of DT is completed, participants don't request for iteration
- Let go with the dynamics of the workshop. Don't be too dogmatic on the approach. Allow for detours, rule breaking in terms of doing things different than the method allows. In this case this is the job (prototype) sharing
- Focus on implementable prototypes: Prototypes can be realistic on the one hand but still too futuristic. With the motivation and the given creativity space, participants tend to define versions ahead.
- Ideas and prototypes can vary. Cross-checks during the prototyping phase against ideas can be beneficial. If there's a difference than the iteration back to ideation should reflect this
- Find a balance between satisfactory level of defining the problem space but also not losing participants through demotivation
- Experiment with solution space and problem space spanning, divergence and convergence cycles and ideation validation with problem space

5   Future Research

The intrinsic motivation and the belief in developing a serious solution to a real business problem have serious positive impacts on the remainder of business.

This is about a transformational observation on how management and overall business of an organization can benefit from DT.

The management increasingly sees value of Design Thinking beyond product and service development. There is valuation of design thinking that replaces typical business thinking. Design Thinking sessions are usually moderated by coaches. There is an advice to research the impact of expert-driven DT coaching versus generic coaches. The hypothesis is that objective experts with design thinking coaching experience can provide more value by challenging the teams than neutral and generic DT coaches. The short-cycle Design Thinking sessions are used to kick-off new project or programs without further researching on the hand-over to development units or teams. The hand-over phase from an idea-prototyping to product generation is not considered in this main research.

→ Prototyping (conceptual/ strategy vs. operational/ product) - design thinking for strategic topics with and without persona must be designed and planned differently

→ DT sessions for short-cycled workshops must be adjusted to the needs of average job function

→ Business and managerial impact of Design Thinking requires further research

References

1. Back, A., Gronau, N., Tochtermann, K. (eds.): Web 2.0 in der Unternehmenspraxis: Grundlagen, Fallstudien und Trends zum Einsatz von Social Software. Oldenbourg Verlag (2012)
2. Bitner, M., Ostrom, A.L., Morgan, F.N.: Service Blueprinting: A Practical Technique For Service Innovation. California Management Review 50(3), 66–94 (2008)
3. Brown, T.: Design Thinking. Harvard Business Review 86(6), 84–92 (2008)
4. Buchenau, M., Suri, J.F.: Experience Prototyping. DIS2000, pp. 424–433. ACM Press, NY (2000)
5. Cigaina, M.: Innovation management framework: Enabling and fostering innovation at enterprises. SAP internal document (to be published by Epistemy Press) (2013)
6. Cooper, R., Junginger, S., Lockwood, T.: Design Thinking and Design Management: A Research and Practice Perspective. Design Management Review 20, 46–55 (2009), doi:10.1111/j.1948-7169.2009.00007.x
7. Coughlan, P., Fulton-Suri, J., Canales, K.: Prototypes as (design) tools for behavioral and organizational change. Journal of Applied Behavioral Science 43, 122–134 (2007)
8. Cross, N.: Designerly ways of knowing. Birkhauser, Boston (2007)
9. Cross, N., Clayburn Cross, A.: Observations of teamwork and social processes in design. Design Studies 16, 143–170 (1995)
10. D.school, Bootcamp Bootleg. Stanford University (2010)

11. Dorst, K., Cross, N.: Creativity in the design process: Co-evolution of problem-solution. Design Studies 22(5), 425–437 (2007)
12. Edvardsson, B., Enquist, B., Johnston, R.: Cocreating customer value through hyperreality in the prepurchase service experience. Journal of Service Research 8(2), 149–161 (2005)
13. Fagerberg, J.: The Oxford Handbook of Innovation. Ox-ford University Press (2006)
14. Gordon, V.S., Bieman, J.M.: Rapid prototyping: lessons learned. IEEE Software 12(1), 85–95 (1995)
15. Hennigs, N., Wiedmann, K.P., Behrens, S., Klarmann, C., Carduck, J.: Brand extensions: A successful strategy in luxury fashion branding? Assessing consumers' implicit associations. Journal of Fashion Marketing and Management 17(4), 390–402 (2013)
16. Hevner, A.R., March, S.T., Park, J., Ram, S.: Design Science in Information Systems Research. MIS Quarterly 28(1), S75–S105 (2004)
17. Hill, R., Hirsch, L., Lake, P., Moshiri, S.: Enterprise Cloud Computing. In: Guide to Cloud Computing, pp. 209–222. Springer, London (2013)
18. Kakabadse, N.K., Kakabadse, A., Ahmed Pervaiz, K.: The ASP phenomenon: an example of solution innovation that liberates organization from technology or captures it? European Journal of Innovation Management 7(2), 113–127 (2004)
19. Kaplan, A.M., Haenlein, M.: Users of the world, unite! The challenges and opportunities of Social Media. Business Horizons 53(1), 59–68 (2010)
20. Klecun, E., Cornford, T.: A Critical Approach to Evaluation. European Journal of IS, 229–243 (2005)
21. Kordon, F.: An introduction to rapid system prototyping. IEEE Transactions on Software Engineering 2002(9), 817–821 (2002)
22. Leonardi, P.M.: Enterprise Social Media: Definition, History, and Prospects for the Study of Social Technologies in Organizations. Journal of Computer-Mediated Communication 19(1) (2013)
23. Lindberg, T., Gumienny, R., Jobst, B., Meinel, C.: Is there a need for a design thinking process. In: Proceedings of the 8th Design Thinking Research Symposium, pp. 243–254. University of Technology, Sydney (2010)
24. March, S.T., Smith, G.: Design and Natural Science Research on Information Technology. Decision Support Systems 15(4), 251–266 (1995)
25. McAfee, A.P.: Enterprise 2.0: The Dawn of Emergent Collaboration. MIT Sloan Management Review 47(3), 21–28 (2006)
26. Meinel, C., Leifer, L., Plattner, H.: Design Thinking: Understand-Improve-Apply. Springer (2011)
27. Newell, A., Shaw, J.C., Simon, H.A.: The process of creative thinking. In: Gruber, H.E., Terrell, G., Wertheimer, M. (eds.) Contemporary approaches to creative thinking, pp. 63–119. Atherton Press, New York (1967)
28. Plattner, H., Meinel, C., Weinberg, U.: Design THiNK!NG – Innovation lernen, Ideenwelten öffnen. mi-Wirtschaftsverlag, München (2009)
29. Ratcliffe, J.: Steps in a design thinking process, pp. 4–4 (2009), https://dschool.stanford.edu/groups/k12/wiki/17cff/ | retrieved April 04, 2013)
30. Schönefeld, F.: Praxisleitfaden Enterprise 2.0: wettbewerbsfähig durch neue Formen der Zusammenarbeit, Kundenbindung und Innovation. Basiswissen zum erfolgreichen Einsatz von Web 2.0-Technologien. Hanser Fachbuchverlag, München (2009)
31. Serie, M.: Imagine. Create. Innovate. Design Thinking with SAP, pp. 27–23 (2012), https://community.wdf.sap.corp/sbs/groups/design-thinkingbts (retrieved March 27, 2013)

32. Shepherd, C., Ahmed, P.K.: From product innovation to solutions innovation: a new paradigm for competitive advantage. European Journal of Innovation Management 3(2), 100–106 (2000)
33. Simon, H.A.: The Sciences of the Artificial, 3rd edn. MIT Press, Cambridge (1996)
34. Tung, W.F., Yuan, S.T.: Idesign: an intelligent design framework for service innovation. In: 40th Annual Hawaii International Conference on System Sciences, HICSS 2007, pp. 64–64. IEEE (January 2007)
35. Vargo, S.L., Lusch, R.F.: Evolving to a New Dominant Logic for Marketing. Journal of Marketing 68, 1–17 (2004)
36. Waloszek, G.: SAP Design Guild: Introduction to design thinking, SAP AG, SAP User Experience, pp. 27–23 (2012), http://www.sapdesignguild.org/community/design/print_design_thinking.asp (retrieved March 27, 2013)
37. Wood, W., Neal, D.T.: A new look at habits and the habit-goal interface. Psychological Review 114(4), 843 (2007)

Business Process Modelling in Design Science Paradigm

Lukasz Ostrowski and Markus Helfert

School of Computing, Dublin City University, Glasnevin, Dublin 9, Ireland
{lostrowski,markus.helfert}@computing.dcu.ie

Abstract. Current challenges in design science research aim for consisting and detailed phases to guide design science researchers to manage projects in the information systems field. By having taken this challenge, we present a reference model, which serves as the foundation to structure information in construction of business process model in design science research. It contains activities responsible for literature review, collaboration with practitioners, and information-modelling. In this paper we focus on the modelling facet to answer a question of how to construct a business process while being invented or created. This is especially applicable when the desired processes do not or only partly exist in organizations. The contribution of the paper is that application of the modelling activities in the context of design science supports the quality of design science artefacts, and provides design science researchers with choices of techniques.

Keywords: Design Science Methodology, BPMN, Top-Down Expansion, Information Quality, Process Modelling.

1   Introduction

Concerning the whole tray of ideas involved what researchers are most impressed by—what they are evidently most interested in—is how the unseen accounts for the seen. Researchers wonder how indefinite motives generate define acts, how indefinite talent creates knowable innovative artefacts, entities that have some separate existence. [1].Innovative ideas are critical for companies and research institutions; however; the process of conducting and initiating innovation is challenging. What has been lacking from previous research is a formalisation of a detailed process to start from an idea and "design" to a valuable output. Design science (DS) research is a prospering paradigm to address this challenge.

Design Science research methodology has received increased attention in computing and information systems (IS) research [2]. It has become an accepted approach for research in the IS discipline, with dramatic growth in related literature [3]. However, its current stage does not offer consisting and comprehending phases, which will guide researchers in their choice of techniques [4]. Thus, in this paper we refer to the reference model which aims for techniques of meta-design artefacts. We discuss and present its modelling step in the context of business process model artefacts.

M. Helfert et al. (Eds.): EDSS 2013, CCIS 447, pp. 111–122, 2014.
© Springer International Publishing Switzerland 2014

This paper is organized as follows. The next section reviews the design science research literature and proposes its challenges and potential ways of further development. Based on that review, the subsequent sections present the reference model that covers phases for meta-design step in DS. Then, we elaborate in depth on one of its phase – modelling, in the context of process oriented artefacts. Next, we evaluate the modelling techniques by means of the Satisfaction Attainment Theory (SAT) [5] and the elaborated solutions. This paper helps define future directions and phases of design science methodology within the full spectrum of information systems research approaches.

2   Design Science Research

Design science focuses on creations of artificial solutions. It addresses research through the *building* and *evaluation* of artefacts designed to meet identified business needs [6]. Understanding the nature and causes of these needs can be a great help in designing solutions [7]. Literature reflects healthy discussion around the balance of rigor and relevance [8] in DS research, which reflects it as a still shaping field [9].

Views and recommendations on the DS methodology vary among papers, e.g. [10,11]. DS methodological guidelines from the precursors Hevner [8] and Walls [12], are seldom 'applied', suggesting that existing methodology is insufficiently clear, or inadequately operationalized - still too high level of abstraction [11]. Descriptions of activities (procedures, tools, techniques) that are needed to follow the methodology are only briefly indicated. By having taken up the challenge, 3 main activities were identified as crucial in the development of DS artefacts [13]. These are: literature review, collaboration with practitioners, and relevant modelling techniques [14]. The reference model [15] examines these activities in terms of development of meta-design artefacts [16]. For a better overview, where it fits in design science methodology, we first introduce our understanding of the current state of the art of DS and its artefacts.

Researchers understand artefacts as "things", i.e. entities that have some separate existence [17]. They can be in form of a construct, model, method, and an instantiation [8]. In construction of the artefact, researchers observed two activity layers [18]: 1) design practice that produces situational design knowledge and concrete artefacts and 2) meta-design that produces abstract design knowledge. " Meta-design can be viewed as 2a) a preparatory activity before situational design is started and 2b) a continual activity partially integrated with the design practice 2c) a concluding theoretical activity summarizing, evaluating and abstracting results directed for target groups outside the studied design and use practices" [18]. The meta-design step concentrates on providing an optimal solution for the domain by trying to cover the whole spectrum. The design practice refers to it, then, by adjusting and applying it to a concrete business scenario (i.e. an instantiation).

As abovementioned, abstract and situational design knowledge can be treated as two individual outcomes of design science. Thus, it seems reasonable to consider two different evaluation methods for each of them; these are – artificial and naturalistic [19].

Meta-design step plays crucial role in constructing the knowledge base for a final instantiation and its utility. Figure 1 illustrates its place in design science research, and the general relationship among IS artefacts [20]. The aim of the reference model was to detail activities [13] that are carried out in that step and then use to guide the design science researchers through it. The three 3 main activities of the reference model were produced by comparing multiple plausible models of reality, which were essential for developing reliable scientific knowledge [21].

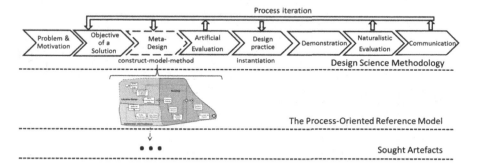

Fig. 1. The Reference model in the Design Science Research Methodology (adapted and updated from Peffers [10])

Next section briefly introduces the insight of the reference model, and how all activities cooperate to achieve a desired solution. Then it elaborates on the process-modelling activities.

3   The Reference Model

The idea behind the reference model is to deliver the knowledge base, which combines information from two processes: literature review and collaboration with practitioners. Their main roles are to 1) gather information related to the investigated domain of interest, and 2) represent the information in an understandable way to the stakeholders. Before analysis and combination of solutions from these sources take place, each process provides its own solution. Thus, to make the analysis and combination part more effective, the same modelling techniques in both processes are introduced. These are the ontology engineering and domain specific modelling language. The former gives researchers the design rationale of a knowledge base, kernel conceptualization of the world of interest, semantic constraints of concepts together with sophisticated theories [22]. In the context of process oriented IS solutions, the latter introduces business process modelling notation (BPMN) [23]. For example, if a researcher investigates a process of an employee engagement, the ontology engineering technique will represent the gathered knowledge retrieved from those two sources. Then, the BPMN will model it into the desired shape of a process. Figure 2 illustrates the overview of the reference model.

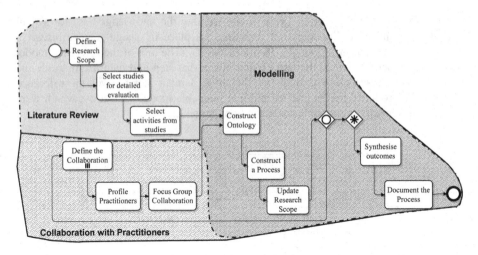

Fig. 2. The Reference Model – Overview [15]

Now, we will describe the modelling task of the reference model. We concentrate on the case where the artefact investigated is a business process model. While we acknowledge this iterative nature of the activities involved, we discuss the model as a linear sequence of steps to keep the description straightforward. We assume to have the knowledge base from the ontology engineering activity and other relevant sources, so a researcher can start modelling the process.

3.1   Construct a Process

We found that BPMN is an appropriate technique to model a business process model in design science paradigm. It provides a graphical notation for specifying business processes and widespread adopted [24]. BPMN is mostly used to construct a representation of an organization's current business processes and its major process variations. In this work are interested in using BPMN to model a process, which doesn't or only partly exists in organizations. The knowledge base produced with the previous steps of the reference model is to contain information to help model it. However, the lack of a full existence of the process model investigated and the need to combine the gather information into one piece makes modelling complicated. BPMN is only a modelling language and does not provide guidelines on how to approach developing or constructing a process in that case. Thus, we decided to reach for a top-down expansion technique [25] using BPMN. The technique starts with an overall picture of the business and continues by analysing each of the process areas of interest. This analysis can be carried out to the precise level of detail required. However, before we elaborate on the steps to achieve the process model of interest, we justify the selection and present the content of BPMN.

3.2   Choosing the Process Notation

The most desirable modelling technique for business processes should be expressive and formal enough but easily understandable also by final users and not only by domain experts faced out. At the present, the state-of-the-art in the field is represented by BPMN [24]. The primary goal of BPMN is to provide a notation that is readily understandable by business users, ranging from the business analysts who sketch the initial drafts of the processes to the technical developers responsible for actually implementing them, and finally to the business staff deploying and monitoring such processes [26].

The advancement of BPMN can be seen through the representational model of Bunge-Wand-Weber ontology (BWW) [27]. This model is understood to contain all necessary constructs to describe things, and the interaction between things, in the real world. In addition it was developed specifically for the IS domain, has a formal specification, and an established track record in the process modelling domain. Also over the last two decades the model has achieved a good level of maturity, adoption and dissemination, allowing considering existing BWW analyses of process modelling languages [28]. Other languages such as Petri-Net (PN) [29], Event Driven Process Chain (EPC) [30], and Integrated Definition Method 3 (IDEF3) [31] were applied to the representational model. The analysis of how these process modelling languages complement each other based on BWW ontology indicated the BPMN as the most appropriate [28]. It is worth noticing that full completeness of BWW representation cannot yet be achieved with the selected languages.

In addition, survey results, conducted on a global scale [32], revealed the practical usage of BPMN business and IT communities. 51% of respondents stated to be using BPMN for business purposes (process documentation, improvement, business analysis, and stakeholder communication) while the remaining 49% used BPMN for more technical purposes (such as process simulation, service analysis and workflow engineering). The popularity of BPMN in can further be seen by looking at sets are being used in practice: 36% of respondents rely on the core BPMN set to develop their (rather basic) process models. 37% use an extended set of BPMN symbols and the remaining 27% use all the functionality BPMN has to offer [32].

3.3   Elements of BPMN

Elements of BPMN can be split into four diagrams: Flow Objects, Connecting Objects, Swimlanes and Artefacts. Flow Objects represent all the actions which can happen inside a business process determining its behaviour. They consist of Events, Activities and Gateways. Connecting Objects provide three different ways of connecting various objects to each other: Sequence Flow, Message Flow and Association. Swimlanes give the capability of grouping the primary modelling elements. Swimlanes have two elements through which modellers can group other elements: Pools and Lanes. Finally, Artefacts are used to provide additional information about a process that does not affect the flow. These are: Data Object, Group, and Annotation [24,23].

Figure 3 illustrates the core elements. For a complete description of BPMN elements and features refer to [22].

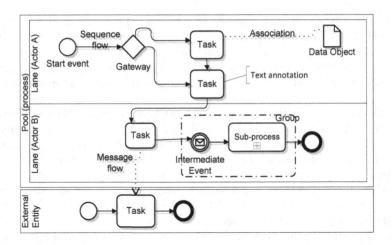

Fig. 3. Business Process Modelling Notation – the Core Elements

3.4   Building the Process Model of Interest

Our approach to build a process is to apply BPMN to the top-down expansion approach [25]. It starts with an overall picture of the process and continues by analysing each of the activity areas of interest. This analysis can be carried out to a precise level of detail required. The level, however, becomes clearer while constructing the process. The process model comprises one or more diagrams. Initially a context diagram is drawn, which is a simple representation of the entire domain under investigation. This is followed by a level 1 diagram identifies the major process at a high level and any of its sub-processes can then be analysed further - giving rise to a corresponding level 2 process diagram. This process of more detailed analysis can then continue – through level 3, 4 and so on. However, most investigations will stop at level 2 and it is very unusual to go beyond a level 3 diagram [25].

Context Diagram. It represents the entire domain under investigation. This diagram is drawn first, and used to clarify and present the scope of the investigation. An example of a context diagram shows Figure 4. The process is represented as a single process, connected to external entities by data objects and message flows. It shows the interfaces between the process under investigation and the external entities with which it communicates. Therefore, whilst it is often conceptually trivial, a context diagram serves to focus attention on the process boundary and can help in clarifying the precise scope of the analysis.

The communication involving external entities are only included where they involve the process. For example, an external entity would communicate with various other entities, which are remote from the process and so this is not included on the context diagram.

To draw a context diagram, firstly we need to draw and name a single pool that represents the entire process. Next, we identify and add the external entities that communicate directly with the process pool. We do this by considering origin and destination of the data objects and message flows. Finally, we add the data objects

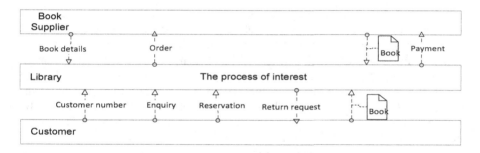

Fig. 4. A Context Diagram with BPMN

and messages flows to the diagram. In drawing the context diagram we only are concerned with the most important information flows. These will be concerned with issues such as: how data objects are received and checked, who does it and to whom is passed.

Process Diagram – Level 1. It shows the main process under investigation. Similarly to the context diagram, any process under investigation should be represented by only one level 1 diagram. There is no formula that can be applied in deciding what is, and what is not, a level 1 process. The level 1 should describe only the main activities of the process, and the temptation of including lower level processes on at this stage should be avoided. As a general rule no business process should contain more than 12 process activities (e.g. tasks, sub-processes) [25]. Figure 5 gives an example of a level 1 process.

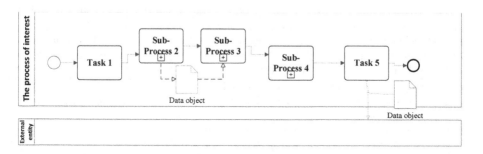

Fig. 5. Business Process Level1

The level 1 diagram is surrounded by Pool that represents the boundaries of the system. Because the level 1 diagram depicts the whole of the system under investigation, it can be difficult to know where to start. There are three different methods, which provide a practical way to start drawing [33]:

• Data Object Analysis may be a useful method for starting the analysis if the process consists largely of the flow of goods, as this approach concentrates on following the flow of physical objects. Data Objects are traced from when they arrive within the boundaries of the process, through the points at which some activity occurs, to their exit from the process. The rationale behind this method is that information will normally flow around the same paths as the physical objects [25].

• Lane Analysis is an approach that starts from an analysis of the main actors (Lanes) that exist within the domain, rather than the goods or information that is flowing around the process. Identification of the key processes results from looking at the domain structure and deciding which processes are relevant to the current Lanes. By looking at these areas in more detail, and analysing what Actors actually do, discrete processes can be identified. Starting with these processes, the information flows between them and between these processes and external entities are then identified and added to the diagram [33].

• Message Flow Analysis [34] approach is appropriate if the part of the business under investigation consists principally of flows of information in the form of computer input and output. Message flow analysis is particularly useful where information flows are of special interest. The first step is to list the major messages and their sources and recipients. This is followed by the identification of other major information flows such as telephone and computer transactions. Once the document flow diagram has been drawn the system boundary should be added.

Further Sub-levels. Whilst there can only be one context and one level 1 diagram for a given process, these normally give rise to numerous lower level diagrams. Each process within a given process diagram may be the subject of further analysis. This involves identifying the lower level processes that together constitute the process of a domain as it was originally identified. As a process diagram is decomposed, each process box becomes a boundary for the next, lower level, process.

To illustrate how it works in practice, three sub-processes were put within the process diagram on Figure 5.Only the outline of the process boxes is shown, which have been identified during the drawing of a level 1 diagram. Any area of a level 1 diagram is likely to require further analysis, as the level 1 diagram itself only provides an overview of the domain. Thus, below the level 1 diagram there will be a series of lower level diagrams. These are referred to as level X+1. However, level 2 is usually sufficient and it is unusual to carry out an analysis beyond level 3. In Figure 6, a sub-process 3 is decomposed further thereby giving rise to a level 2 diagram [33].

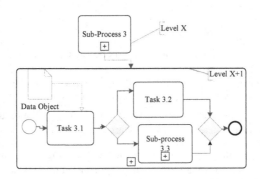

Fig. 6. Level 2 Process Diagram: Sub-levels

In the level 2 diagram three activities of interest have been identified and the numbering of these processes must reflect the parent process-3.1, 3.2, and 3.3. If we assume that one activity (e.g. sub-process 3.3) within this was of sufficient interest and complexity to justify further analysis, we could then further analyse resulting in a corresponding level 3 diagram. Once again the numbering of these processes must reflect the parent process. Therefore these three level 3 activities would be numbered 3.3.1, 3.3.2, and so on.

It is important to know when to stop the process of top-down expansion. Usually this will be at level 2 or level 3. There are three useful guidelines to help you to decide when to stop the analysis [33]:

• A process has a single input flow or a single output flow then it should be apparent that there is little point in analysing it any further.
• A process is accurately described by a single active verb with a singular object; this also indicates that the analysis has been carried out to a sufficiently low level. For example, the process named validate enquiry contains a single discrete task.
• If anything useful will be gained by further decomposition of a process, the question is whether it would influence any further process decisions. If the answer is no, then there is little point in taking the analysis further.

Clarity of a Model. We already introduced the explicitness of the hierarchical decomposition of a process as an aspect of the process modelling. The comprehensibility of the process layout design concerns the graphical arrangement of the information objects, and, therefore, supports the rationality of a model. There is a variety of simple techniques to show how a process diagram can be clarified and easily read by users. One is, where a diagram is considered to contain too many processes, those that are related can often be combined. As a general rule no process diagram should contain more than 12 activities. In some examples multiple activities can be identified as being related and can be combined into a single task with a collective description. Other technique is where information is being retrieved from a data object, and it is not necessary to show the selection criteria, or key, that is being used to retrieve it. Where a data object is being updated, only the data flow representing the update needs to be shown. The fact that the information must first be retrieved does not need to be shown. Only the most important reports, enquiries, are needed to be on the diagram. Communications that are of less significance can, if necessary, be detailed in support documentation.

4   Evaluation of the Modelling Activities

The modelling activities were evaluated from three different perspectives: perceived net goal attainment, satisfaction with the outcome as well as satisfaction with the process. These three perspectives constitute the Satisfaction Attainment Theory which was used with participants who conducted these activities and were asked to elaborate on the business process model artefacts modelled. Participants of these activities were stakeholders of a public organisation. The organisation provided IT services for various departments. The practitioners in the numbers of 7 were between 29-58 years of age (M 43, SD 3.4). The gender was split in 5 males, and 2 females. Their work experience in the organisation was between 0.5 to 12 years (M 5, SD 1.3). They role mainly were engineers from fields of electronics, design, architecture, and computing. Participants took part in these activities willingly, and therefore, it was assumed their responses to the questionnaire were genuine.

Table 1 summarizes the results of the evaluation of the meeting satisfaction. We used 11-point Likert questions (11=best), relating to each of the elements of the Satisfaction Attainment Theory.

Table 1. Evaluation of the modelling activities

Dimension	Mean	n
Perceived Net Goal Attainment (PGA)	9.3	7
Satisfaction with the Process (SP)	10.6	7
Satisfaction with the Outcome (SO)	9.9	7

The values for the means indicate a high satisfaction of the participants with each of the three dimensions from the Satisfaction Attainment Theory. Each element was measured by five questions in the questionnaire. All fifteen questions can be found in the appendix A of [5].

The business process artefacts built with the modelling activities of the reference model scored explicitly as well as the process of execution the modelling activities. This concludes the usage of the model for the main purpose, which was to provide researchers with a structure way to help conduct and communicate the research outcome with the stakeholders. We claim that the modelling activities of the reference model constitute a consistent method for the meta-design phase in design science research methodology to guide the design science researchers to manage information systems projects.

5   Conclusion

We observed challenges in structuring and standardizing phases of design science research methodology, which would guide the design science researchers in their choices of techniques that might be appropriate at each stage of the project and also help them plan, manage, control and evaluate information systems projects. We introduced how to construct a business process model using BPMN in the context of design science methodology. The activities outlined were a part of a reference model that helps structure and model knowledge in design science research

Our future work involves revising the model, based on users' feedback, and concentrating on evaluation techniques of its outcome. Hopefully, this will increase the efficiency and quality of artefacts, while containing or further decreasing the cognitive effort involved.

Acknowledgments. This work was supported by the Irish Research Council under the Enterprise Partnership Scheme.

References

1. Fishman, N.: Viral Data in SOA: An Enterprise Pandemic. IBM Press, New York City (2009)
2. Kuechler, B., Vaishnavi, V.: On Theory Development in Design Science Research: Anatomy of a Research Project. Europeam Journal of Information Systems 17(5), 489–504 (2008)
3. Carlsson, S.A., Henningsson, S., Hrastinski, S., Keller, C.: Socio-technical IS design science research: developing design theory for IS integration management. Information Systems and E-Business Management 9(1), 109–131 (2011)
4. Alturki, A., Gable, G.G., Bandara, W.: A Design Science Research Roadmap. In: Jain, H., Sinha, A.P., Vitharana, P. (eds.) DESRIST 2011. LNCS, vol. 6629, pp. 107–123. Springer, Heidelberg (2011)
5. Briggs, R.O., Reinig, B.A., de Vreede, G.-J.: Meeting satisfaction for tech-supported groups: an empirical validation of a goal-attainment model. Small Group Research 36, 585–611 (2006)
6. Hevner, A.R., March, S.T., Park, J., Ram, S.: Design Science in Information Systems Research. MIS Quarterly 28, 75–106 (2004)
7. Van Aken, J.E.: Management Research as a Design Science: Articulating the Research Products of Mode 2 Knowledge Production in Management. British Journal of Management 16(1), 19–36 (2005)
8. Hevner, A.R., March, S.T., Park, J., Ram, S.: Design Science in Information Systems Research. MIS Quarterly 28, 75–106 (2004)
9. Iivari, J., Venable, J.: Action research and design science research–seemingly similar but decisively dissimilar. In: 17th European Conference on Information Systems (2009)
10. Baskerville, R., Pries-Heje, J., Venable, J.: Soft Design Science Methodology. In: DESRIST 2009, Malvern (2009)
11. Peffers, K., Tuunanen, T., Rothenberger, M.: A Design Science Research Methodology. Journal of Management Information Systems 24(3), 45–77 (2007)
12. Walls, J., Widmeyer, G., El Sawy, O.: Building an Information System Design Theory for Vigilant EIS. Information Systems Research 3(1), 36–59 (1992)
13. Ostrowski, L., Helfert, M., Xie, S.: A Conceptual Framework to Construct an Artefact for Meta-Abstract Design. In: Sprague, R. (ed.) 45th Hawaii International Conference on Systems Sciences, Maui, pp. 4074–4081 (2012)
14. Ostrowski, Ł., Helfert, M., Hossain, F.: A Conceptual Framework for Design Science Research. In: Grabis, J., Kirikova, M. (eds.) BIR 2011. LNBIP, vol. 90, pp. 345–354. Springer, Heidelberg (2011)
15. Ostrowski, L., Helfert, M.: Reference Model in Design Science Research to Gather and Model Information. In: 18th Americas Conference on Information Systems, Seattle (2012)
16. Walls, J., Widmeyer, G., El Sawy, O.: Building an Information System Design Theory for Vigilant EIS. Information Systems Research 3(1), 36–59 (1992)
17. Goldkuhl, G.: Design Theories in Information Systems – A Need for Multi-Grounding. Journal of Information Technology and Application 6(2), 59–72 (2004)
18. Goldkuhl, G., Lind, M.: A Multi-Grounded Design Research Process. In: Winter, R., Zhao, J.L., Aier, S. (eds.) DESRIST 2010. LNCS, vol. 6105, pp. 45–60. Springer, Heidelberg (2010)
19. Pries-Heje, J., Baskerville, R., Venable, J.: Strategies for Design Science Research Evaluation. In: 16th European Conference on Information Systems, pp. 255–266 (2008)

20. Gregor, S., Jones, D.: The Anatomy of a Design Theory. Journal of Assoc. Information Systems 8, 312–335 (2007)
21. Azevedo, J.: Mapping Reality: An Evolutionary Realist Methodology for the Natural and Social Sciences, Albany (1997)
22. Mizoguchi, R.: Tutorial on Ontological Engineering. New Generation Computing 21(4), 363–384 (2003)
23. OMG: Business Process Modelling Notation, http://www.omg.org/spec/BPMN/2.0/ (accessed March 2012)
24. Chinosi, M., Trombetta, A.: BPMN: An introduction to the standard. Computer Standards & Interfaces 34(1), 123–134 (2012)
25. Chester, M., Athwall, A.: Basic Information Systems Analysis and Design. McGraw-Hill (2002)
26. White, S.A.: BPMN 1.0 Business Process Notation - OMG Final Adopted Specification, http://www.bpmn.org (accessed May 2011)
27. Weber, R.: Ontological Foundations of Information Systems Monograph. Coopers & Lybrand, Melbourne (1997)
28. Muehlen, Z.M., Indulska, M.: Modeling Languages for Business Processes and Business Rules: A Representational Analysis. Information Systems 35(4), 379–390 (2010)
29. Petri, C.A.: Kommunikation mit Automaten, vol. 2. Institut für Instrumentelle Mathematik, Universität Bonn, Bonn (1962)
30. Scheer, A.-W.: ARIS - Business Process Modelling. Springer (1999)
31. Mayer, R., Menzel, C., Painter, M., Perakath, B., Dewitte, P., Blinn, T.: Information Integration For Concurrent Engineering (IICE) - IDEF3 Process Description Capture Method Report. Technical Report (1995), http://www.idef.com/pdf/idef3_fn.pdf
32. Recker, J.: BPMN Modeling - Who, where, How and Why, http://www.sparxsystems.com/press/articles/pdf/bpmn_survey.pdf (accessed March 2012)
33. ITT Ltd: GetAhead in Business Analysis Data Flow Diagrams. ITT Ltd (2009)
34. Nierstrasz, O.M.: Message Flow Analysis. PhD Thesis CSRI Technical Report #165, Department of computer Science, University of Toronto, Toronto (1984)

Sustaining IT Usefulness – Re-defining End Users' Role as Contextual Designers

Nathan Lakew

Mid Sweden University, Sundsvall, SE
nathan.lakew@miun.se

Abstract. A framework for understanding and interpreting IT usefulness and fitness attributes is presented. This framework is grounded on a relationship that exists between organisms and their landscape. The concept draws on the notion that sustainable relationship between two systems (such as IT and end-users) can be achieved through structural coupling results from mutual perpetuations. In this setting, while contextual usefulness is established in the end-users' environment, IT designers perpetuate fitness into the conceptual environment. Their relationship suggests that usefulness feeds essential input that enables to create a sustainable fitness attribute. Based on the empirical evidence, the paper demonstrates that end-users are better equipped with defining contextual *usefulness* of IT systems while IT designers' role to create fitness attribute enables a long-term use of IT artifacts.

Keywords: Usefulness, Fitness, structural coupling, conceptual and contextual space.

1 Introduction

Recently, IS research "has found its legitimacy" [1] in the design science research where the main focus has been designing artifacts in the form of methods, instantiations and IT systems. However, literature that are specifically concerns with developing guidelines to design IT artifacts [2-4] recognized that the process of developing an IT artifact will not be finalized once it is appropriated by end-users. In fact, the success of IT artifacts are subjected to rigorous "quality evaluation and efficacy" [2] in post-implementation.

As Gill and Hevner [5] point out, IS research has been widely used IT artifact's usefulness attribute as the main evaluation criteria for IT success[6]. In this setting, IT is mainly evaluated based on functions and properties it possesses to match end-users' requirements. But recent research [7, 8] has shown that end-users' environment is always in the course of change where organizations are portrayed as 'self-design' [8] systems. To sustain IT systems' usefulness, IS design practice needs what Gill and Hevner[5] referred to as a fitness attribute that involves adaption and evolution of IT artifacts.

The purpose of this paper is to illustrate the application of fitness attribute to sustain the usefulness of IT artifacts. The paper develops an analytical framework to

M. Helfert et al. (Eds.): EDSS 2013, CCIS 447, pp. 123–134, 2014.

demonstrate the relationship between these two attributes and their figurative domain space. Based on the analytical framework, the paper questions end-users' role in the process of IS design which is traditionally limited to requirements knowledge base. It draws on a case study of newly implemented Learning Management System (LMS) called Moodle at Mid Sweden University in three different campuses. The study includes an in-depth interview with the so-called Moodle champions, who were responsible for the smooth transition of LMS in their perspective departments, IT developers' team, Moodle deployment project administrators, and Learning Resource Center (LRC).

Organization of the Paper: First a summary of IS literature that concerns with long-term use of IT systems is presented as a theoretical background. Second, conceptual founding of fitness and usefulness attributes in IS design will be presented. Third, based on the conceptual foundation, an analytical framework is developed to illustrate the relationship between these two attributes. Finally, after presenting a case study, I further discuss these attributes and their contribution toward long-term use of IT artifacts.

2 Theoretical Foundation

With regard to IS practice that aims for a long-term use of IT systems, a number of researchers proposed different methods, conceptual frameworks, and IS design theories. However, much of the work focused on IS practices that occurs after the deployment of IT systems. Such IT practices mainly include, but are not limited to, rigorous evaluating mechanisms of IT artifacts and robust IT training programs.

Mendoza et al.[9], for example, report that the role of usefulness in the process of adopting and adapting technology fades once end-users become what the authors referred to as long-termer users. After the initial adoption, long-termer users' focus shifts from technology features that satisfy functionality needs to features that enable users to manipulate the technology to suit their ever-changing work practices. After initial adoption, new aspects of usefulness emerges that concern with the ability of a system to facilitate exploring and constructing new work practice. The authors argue that well-established and on-going IT trainings play a crucial role to sustain a long-term usefulness of IT artifacts.

Tyre and Orlikowski [10] developed a model to describe different stages that a technology will go through during IT implementation. With three different cases they have presented, the authors consistently observed that end-users' effort to adapt a technology into their daily activities gradually diminishes as routine gets its way. Initial adaption to technology mainly aims to routinize technology with daily activities than aiming for using artifacts for long-term use. But subsequent adaptions triggered by different events such as new work practices can lead to finding ways to sustain usefulness of an IT artifact. Tyre and Orlikowski's model highlights enabling and constraining factors that influence adaption, most of which are associated with the process of new IT system adoption.

Carroll et al.[11] introduced Model of technology Appropriation (MTA) to describe the appropriation process they claim to include long-term use of IT artifacts.

MTA describes technology appropriation at three levels: when it is adopted and evaluated based on its usefulness, when it becomes routinized and adapted to existing work practices, and when it is considered stabilized and enforced as a result of technology entanglements with existing practices. At times, the authors suggested, endusers' activities can change and these changes affect technology's way of being from 'technology-as-designed' to 'technology-in-use'. They concluded that long-term use IT artifacts' factors are 'unlikely to be uncover' with the usually short and targeted tests organized in the beginning of new IT system's adoption.

The above exemplars of technology appropriation and long-term use of IT systems research show that there is a general consensus regarding the relationship between the initial usefulness of IT artifacts and the success of long-term use. End-users' practice of adapting technology to the existing work practice is mainly based on the usefulness attribute of IT artifacts. In addition, users' active participation seemed to slow down as technology properly placed in existing practice. However, it is still unclear how, in the process of IS design, IS designers can inset attributes that sustain the usefulness of IT artifacts to create long-term use technology.

In exploring this research question, the paper grounds on Gill and Hevner [5] work, who show that IS design can have two focus, a fitness or a usefulness focus. The authors [5] present a fitness-utility model to describe the evolving nature of IT artifacts. Usefulness is presented as having a close tie with other prominent IS researches which consider usefulness as being both a motivation factor and evaluation criteria to select and adopt IT systems. Fitness-utility model is presented as complementary to the well-established usefulness model in describing the adaptive attributes of artifacts.

3 Conceptual Foundation of Fitness and Usefulness Attributes

Gill and Hevner [5] suggest that usefulness in its broadest term embodies IT systems' characteristics such as "efficacy in performing the task (including performance), range of task cases performed, ease of use, ease of learning, and cost-benefit in the performance of a task". Here usefulness represents all IT artifacts' attributes that are related to task performance.

Central to usefulness is the task of defining design candidates in the design space. Requirements are searched for a viable design candidate. The well-established Cartesian world view [12] informs the search for design candidates. In this view, end-users' needs (specific design candidates) are thought to be 'representational' and can be segmented to the level of operational ends. Once the design candidate's goal is represented in a specific form, the next step is to convert these goals to 'constraints and functions' using IT artifacts.

Gill and Hevner [5] suggested two circumstances where the word fitness can be applied. The first definition is related to its use in the evolution field. Here, fitness of an organism represents its ability to continuously reproduce and evolve for successive generations. The second definition of fitness implies to a shorter and specific fitness scenarios. For example, an organism's ability to overcome a specific situation or danger in a given period of time makes it fit to that specific situation. Individual physical fitness for a specific type of sport can be a good example to the second definition of fitness. In this paper the word fitness refers to the first definition that concern with the evolving ability of IT artifacts for the purpose of sustaining usefulness. Hence, design that focuses on fitness aims to develop the competency of IT artifacts' evolving and adapting ability in users' environment.

A closer look on how organism creates a long-term fitness can be used to illustrate the relationship between fitness and usefulness. Biological organisms do not create *representations* of their environment in order to adapt with it. In fact, their environment is too complex to be represented. Instead, their interaction can be described as patterns of practices that continuously change their own *structure* to adapt their landscape. Maturana and Guiloff [14] describes this interaction using the concept of structural coupling:

> When two or more plastic dynamic systems interacts recursively under conditions in which their identities are maintained, the process of structural coupling takes place as a process of reciprocal selection of congruent paths of structural changes in the interacting systems … [14], p. 139

The definition draws on the idea that two plastic systems can mutually affect each other continuously or at least one repeatedly perturbs the other. A plastic system represents one that can be affected by external events (e.g. organism or environment). The mutual perpetuation of systems (e.g. organisms, software, environment) "leads to a structural fit between the systems" [15].

Each structure is created as a result of perturbed activities, which in turn continuously change perturbation domain (e.g. design space). Fitting to unyielding environment is not a matter of information process or representation of contextual details. Organisms change their *structure* to respond to perturbed changes. The transformation in structure is important to generate an "appropriate change of state triggered by specific perturbing changes" [16]. The process of change in structure, in turn, is affected by the perturbing changes. That is, specific details and changes gradually create "history of responses" [16] leading up to structural formation.

On the one hand, usefulness is specifically concerned with contextual responses where *operational* level fitness is materialized. End-users are the main actors in this activity as they are closer to the application domain. On the other hand, fitness facilitates the contextual respond by providing a plat-form or structure at a conceptual level. Design that targets a long-term use of IT artifact, thus, focuses on the structure of the artifact than the contextual usefulness of it.

Fitness sees each usefulness demarcations of design candidates as instantiation of users' needs. What usefulness focused IS design assumes to be a design candidate is just another 'temporal regularity' [7] in the eyes of fitness focused IS design. In this sense, fitness can be called instantiations of usefulness. Even though, fitness provides a means to guarantee usefulness, the reverse does not hold true. Structural coupling is the bases for both selection and evolution [16]. While selection of an individual organism depends on surviving each given unyielding circumstance at a time, evolution requires a continuous coupling with other autopoiesis. Structural coupling guarantees both temporal (usefulness) and co-evolutionary situations. Even though, fixing temporal regularities considered essential in the fitness landscape, it is not a sufficient condition for sustaining usefulness.

Hence fitness aims to design sustainable affordances that are malleable to the general design space. Temporary regularities are seen as just another opportunity for a more structural coupling. Usefulness continuously feeds essential input to fitness. There is a feed-back loop like mechanism (described as activities in the analytical framework below) where the structure affects the response and vice versa. In addition, an explanation as to where these two activities are realized can be characterized in two abstract domains: conceptual domain (structure level) and contextual domain (response level). The next section further elaborates the relationship between fitness and usefulness using analytical framework.

4 Analytical Framework

The purpose this framework (See figure 4.1) is to demonstrate the application of fitness and usefulness attributes in designing IT artifacts. The framework can be used as analytical tool to identify, organize, and interpret essential activities that involves IS design practices and end users' interaction with IT systems.

Defining Space

One of the key assumptions in the framework is that there existing two spaces that the IS practice operates: contextual and conceptual. In the contextual space, end users and implementers strive to embed technological properties and functions to their context. Here, the main goal is to achieve contextual affordances using IT artifact functions and properties. Contextual space represents end-users environment that is emergent and complex in nature. Conceptual space oversees 'perturbed activities' and provide structure that facilitates fitness based on the feedback from contextual space. In other word, conceptual space provides a means for successful structural coupling between users and their context. In doing so, it does not concern with specific users context or particular affordances. While IS design that focuses on usefulness tries to find representable design candidate within contextual space, fitness focused design leave the allocation of affordances for end-users. This way, end-users are able to define both problems and solutions based on their context.

Activities – Embedding and De-embedding

There are two activities in the analytical framework represented by arrows in fig. 4. While the embedding activity arrow shows the creation of contextual affordances to specific needs, de-embedding activity represents the process of 'abstracting' general rules [17] to create coupling ability for the artifact.

Embedding represents the process of "place-making" [18] new technological artifacts to existing work practice. End users and implementers are considered to be actors of this process. End-users assemble and scramble affordances accordingly with their context. This is also in line with the framework of Maturana's structural coupling, where organisms use all available means to survive and continue to fit in a landscape. End-users design contextual 'placement' of IT artifacts and become 'secondary designers' on their own terms.

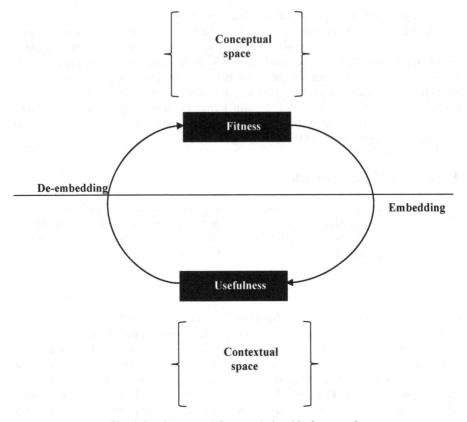

Fig. 1. Usefulness and fitness relationship framework

As a result of embedding 'design', new work practices can emergent. These work practices, including workarounds, are matured toward contextual usefulness. New work practices can be taken as new IS opportunities/problems that need a fitness 'touch'. That is, IS developers may decide to include coupling mechanism for these new practices in their next 'version'. Thus, de-embedding activities trigged to create technological properties and functions to sustain new contextual affordances.

Crossing the Imaginary Threshold between Conceptual and Contextual Space

There is no defined starting point for any design [17]. Different actors play important roles in defining the threshold of these imaginary spaces and activities. In this analytical framework, implementers or sometimes called super-users can share both the embedding and de-embedding activities with developers and end-users. In a sense, they are the mediators for different 'spaces'. The setting is depend on the organizational strategy, IS design architecture, and other IS method of development issues. Reflecting on the case study that is presented in this manuscript, super-users were used to implement new technology, where developers were continuously adding new functions and properties.

5   Case Study

The paper draws on a case study of newly implemented Learning Management System (LMS) called Moodle at Mid Sweden University in three different campuses. The study includes an in-depth interview with the so-called Moodle champions, who were responsible for the smooth transition of LMS in their perspective departments, IT developers' team, Moodle deployment project administrators, and Learning Resource Center (LRC). Currently Moodle serves more than 17,000 students and the university's 1500 staff under the supervision of Learning Management Center (LRC).

Research Method

The university has nominated 16 Moodle champions, tasked with supporting the implementation process of Moodle. With the permission of LRC, nine Moodle champions were agreed to participate in an in-depth interview, each lasts between 30-60 minutes. In addition, 5 more LRC staffs (2 Moodle developers, 1 LRC staff and 2 LRC administrators) have participated in the interview. In total, 14 interviewees were participated in the span of 6 month data collection. It should be noted that a follow-up interview has been conducted to three LRC staffs.

Data were collected using tape recordings and notes. All interviews were transcript to Atlas.ti. Descriptive codes were applied to categorized patterns and specific themes. In coding the data, 'content analysis' [19] method is used to examine transcript interviews at the conversation level. The main objective of the analysis was to explore IS practices that affect long-term use of IT artifacts. Two different level of IS practices are emerged from the analysis. A third activity, feed-back loop, is presented as a theme that communicates these IS practices (see table 5.1). In particular, the following steps were followed:

1) All the interviews are transcribed and uploaded to Atlas.ti software

2) After re-reading all the interviews, 20% of coding have been done manual. In doing so, patterns were observed at conversation level.

3) After coding each response, the author examined IS practices and corresponding actors in each of the coded conversations. Three main activities (families as Atlas.ti calls it) have emerged (See table 3). Each family was then compared with the interviewees response based on the original code.

4) Based on these families, the paper develops logical relationship with the analytical framework in discussing the findings.

6   Findings

The analysis of the case study allows illustrating the relationship between usefulness and fitness attributes and the application of the analytical framework. While end-users' practices are illustrated in the contextual domain, IT developers' and LRC staffs' activities are represented in the conceptual level of IS practice.

Table 1. Three Main categories emerged from coding

Categories	Descriptions	Examples	Actors
Conceptual Level activities	IT designers inset fitness attribute on to sustain useful-ness	*"If we feel like it is important (functionality) and a decision is made here in LRC"*	LRC staffs and Moodle champions
Contextual Level activities	End-users continu-ously define both design candidates and contextual affordances using IT functions and properties.	*"I have workaround as well, which I created before long time ago, from WebCT limita-tion, but I continue using it, in fact I adapted my old solution (to) the new system"*	End-users' and Moodle champions
Feed-back mechanism	Both IT designers and end-users exchange input for usefulness and fitness.	*"We sent our complaints and raise the issue in the champi-on meetings"*	Moodle champions

Embedding Practices: Creating Contextual Usefulness

Before Moodle was rolled-out, champions from each department were participated in training workshops to learn how to modify and create affordances accordingly with their respective departments' need. Such affordances mainly include department based forms, subject based data uploading mechanisms (e.g. math numeric assign-ments), section forms that introduce courses, subject based student forms. In the be-ginning of Moodle implementation, champions were asked to provide IT affordances that suits the existing practice (*"I used to get question like 'would it be good if I can do this' then I would say, but yes you can do that" Tagged 04 (...) "The question is more about the equivalent options they can get in Moodle." Tagged06*). End-users' past entanglements with technological practices are found to be the main driving force of defining new contextual usefulness.

In addition, contextual affordances are found to be emergent and locally confined. Different course given in different seasons, teachers' transfer, organizational changes in departments, introduction of new courses are few list of reasons that are continu-ously emerge as a new contextual requirements. Moodle champions were constantly changing local artifacts' usefulness and teach end-users to create those contextual affordances. (*"There is always discussion about how to design for different types of courses regarding to the subject and/or if it is a campus or a distance form. Chal-lenges come(s) every week" Tagged 12 (...) "They often tell me "but I'll keep that example from the template just in case I need it later", and get surprised when I show them how easy it is to delete it and create it all over again. I think people are used to the fact that the WebCT structure was not as malleable, and since they are not aware of how easy it is to modify things in Moodle" Tagged 04.*)

The data also reveal that end-users are proven to be competent designers of their own contextual environment. Contextual affordances may sometimes involve partial use of IT artifacts' function, while workarounds affixed to fill the rest. On this regard, users competently assembled fragments of affordances both from technological functions and perceptual artifacts (workarounds). *"The great limitation is you can't attach files to emails. In my department, the architects want to upload files but then I have to send those from outlook, so it is hard. We find some way around it, we instead start to use a forum to upload the files, but I don't think that is efficient way to do it" Tagged 05).*

De-embedding Practices: Creating Conceptual Fitness

In the quest of creating contextual affordances, users continuously entangles context with IT artifacts' functionalities. As a result, new requirements were continuously emerged. Moodle champions received different functionality requirements and if necessary let the LRC staffs aware of these new requirements. The case study shows that such requirements were handled to enhance Moodle functions and properties.

First, users' requirement is de-embed from contextual use to develop context neutral IT artifact functions. LRC administrators make the final decision whether to append (in most cases, plug-ins) such functionalities or not. *("If we feel like it is important and a decision is made here in LRC" Tagged 03).* Secondly, LRC administrators also decided whether such functionalities should be available for all departments. In a way, contextual environment feeds the IT artifacts' structure to continuously evolve with emergent needs.

Feed-Back Loop – Communication between Conceptual and Contextual Space

Moodle champions were playing the role of a 'middleman' between LRC staffs and end-users to create a feed-back loop between usefulness and fitness *("We sent our complaints and raise the issue in the champion meetings" tagged 09).* Even though, such settings are existed, the case study also shown that there were not used effectively (*"Process from the universities is not usually specific. For example, they goes like Facebook works better, but they don't say what is they need that is similar to Facebook that needs to be there. The request is not correct and the way it comes is not standard as well. Sometimes it comes to me and other times it goes to the LRC" tagged 02).*

In summary, it is evident from the case study that contextual (usefulness) and structural (fitness) changes are implemented in different level of domain space; at conceptual and contextual space. In addition, the analysis has shown that end-users' role as contextual designers can provide competent feedback for long-term use of IT artifacts.

7 Discussion and Conclusion

In this paper, I set out to illustrate the application of fitness attribute to sustain the usefulness of IT artifacts. The paper develops an analytical framework to demonstrate the relationship between these two attributes and their figurative domain space. I argue that while both attributes play an essential role in developing sustainable IT artifacts, fitness based IS design slightly questions traditionally assigned roles given to IT designers and end-users.

On the one hand, conceptual space is used to demonstrate IT designers' role as contextual affordance facilitators. In this capacity, designers are expected to continuously instill the fitness attributes based on the feedback from end-users' IT practices. On the other hand, contextual space is defined as end-users' environment where particulars or daily context based affordances are continuously created and scrapped. Permanent affordances, then, can be used as a candidate for fitness attribute. It is argued that users are competent to analysis and define their own contextual affordances in a coherent manner. Implementers/super users play an important role in the process of embedding IT systems in the contextual environment. The case study presented in this paper demonstrates these relationships. In addition, it is shows that end-users can deliver constrictive feedback that can be used as a base to continuously produce fitness attribute for existing IT system.

Naturally, usefulness focused IS design bases on a finely developed requirement specifications and particulars results from a well-defined methodological engineering steps [20]. The rationale behind such effort is that well-defined requirement elicitations results a finely tuned IT artifacts with users' environment. IS literature have documented that solutions developed based on design methods that promote 'specific fitness of user-requirement' failed to adapt once they are appropriated by users [21-23]. This is because, as noted previously, end-users' environment is full of articulations and negotiations that may or may not involve IT artifacts. It is implausible to capture all such socio-technical entanglements in a specific timeframe of user requirement analysis. The more a designer focuses on specifics and particulars, the more it misses the holistic user environment that includes socio-technical 'imbrications' [24] such as workarounds and locally implemented work practices. Hence, the rationale behind the emphasis of usefulness may actually result in working against the very design reasoning behind the usefulness of an IT artifact. That is, an overemphasis on the usefulness can result in a less useful IT artifact.

The paper has also emphasized end-users' input for IT artifacts' fitness attribute. The process by which end-users implement, and at times modify, IT artifacts has been referred to as 'secondary design' [25]. In this setting, primary design demarcates the design process to develop IT systems' properties and functions. An IS design that emphasizes the importance of developing usefulness attribute at the outset leaves less room for secondary design, thus limits the evolving attribute or fitness of IT systems. Design that focus on the fitness attribute transfers the responsibility of defining problem space and creating contextual affordances to the hands of end-users. The assumption is that design candidate in users' environment kept changing contextually and cannot be defined at the outset. Since end-users' environment is considered to be socio-technical, the practice of design, ontologically, falls in the holistic tradition.

In addition, the strong association between usefulness and IT success criteria indirectly affects the search process of a design candidate during users' requirement elicitation. In defining user requirements, usefulness obliged the searching process to be focused on design candidates that can be formulated as a "structure of goals" [26]. Hence, system analysts see users' environment as field of problems that can be converted to operational ends. As it is stated, however, ends are not always clear, but "must be constructed from messy problems"[27] or sometimes called "wicked problems" [28]. The application of usefulness logic to define wicked IS problems as operational ends can result in a short-term use of IT systems.

As contemporary organizations are increasingly becoming complex and their needs are being portrayed as instable[29], applying usefulness at the outset to develop, adopt and evaluate IT artifacts can be limiting. It is factual that the relevance of any product, first and foremost, depends on its contextual usefulness. But predicting contextual usefulness, even as situational practices or as design-in-use, at the outset can affect long-term use of IT artifacts. The findings in this paper advocate end-users' competency to define their own contextual affordances, thus shifting such IT practices into the hands of end-users.

References

1. Hovorka, D., Germonprez, M.: Tinkering, tailoring and bricolage: Implications for theories of design. In: Proceedings of the 15th Americas Conference on Information Systems (2009)
2. Hevner, A.R., et al.: Design science in information systems research. MIS Quarterly 28(1), 75–105 (2004)
3. March, S.T., Storey, V.C.: Design science in the information systems discipline: an introduction to the special issue on design science research. MIS Quarterly 32(4), 725–730 (2008)
4. Peffers, K., et al.: A design science research methodology for information systems research. Journal of Management Information Systems 24(3), 45–77 (2007)
5. Gill, T.G., Hevner, A.R.: A fitness-utility model for design science research. In: Jain, H., Sinha, A.P., Vitharana, P. (eds.) DESRIST 2011. LNCS, vol. 6629, pp. 237–252. Springer, Heidelberg (2011)
6. Delone, W.H.: The DeLone and McLean model of information systems success: a ten-year update. Journal of Management Information Systems 19(4), 9–30 (2003)
7. Truex, D.P., Baskerville, R., Klein, H.: Growing systems in emergent organizations. Commun. ACM 42(8), 117–123 (1999)
8. Weick, K.E., Sutcliffe, K.M., Obstfeld, D.: Organizing and the process of sensemaking. Organization Science 16(4), 409–421 (2005)
9. Mendoza, A., Carroll, J., Stern, L.: Adoption, adaption, stabilization and stagnation: software appropriation over time. In: ACIS 2005. University of Technology, Sydney (2005)
10. Tyre, M.J., Orlikowski, W.J.: Windows of opportunity: Temporal patterns of technological adaptation in organizations. Organization Science 5(1), 98–118 (1994)
11. Carroll, J., et al.: A field study of perceptions and use of mobile telephones by 16 to 22 year olds. Journal of Information Technology Theory and Application (JITTA) 4(2), 6 (2002)
12. Descartes, R.: The philosophical writings of Descartes, vol. 2. Cambridge University Press (1985)
13. Stefanou, C.J.: A framework for the ex-ante evaluation of ERP software. European Journal of Information Systems 10(4), 204–215 (2001)
14. Maturana, H.R., Guiloff, G.D.: The quest for the intelligence of intelligence. Journal of Social and Biological Structures, 1980 3(2), 135–148 (1980)
15. Quick, T., et al.: The essence of embodiment: A framework for understanding and exploiting structural coupling between system and environment. In: AIP Conference Proceedings (2000)

16. Winograd, T.A., Flores, C.F.: Understanding computers and cognition: A new foundation for design. Ablex Pub (1986)
17. Lee, J.S., Pries-Heje, J., Baskerville, R.: Theorizing in design science research. In: Jain, H., Sinha, A.P., Vitharana, P. (eds.) DESRIST 2011. LNCS, vol. 6629, pp. 1–16. Springer, Heidelberg (2011)
18. Riemer, K., Johnston, R.B.: Place-making: A Phenomenological Theory of Technology Appropriation (2013)
19. Klein, H.K., Truex, D.P.: Discourse analysis: a semiotic approach to the investigation of organizational emergence. The Semiotics of the Workplace (1995)
20. Iivari, J., Hirschheim, R., Klein, H.K.: A paradigmatic analysis contrasting information systems development approaches and methodologies. Information Systems Research 9(2), 164–193 (1998)
21. DeSanctis, G., Poole, M.S.: Capturing the Complexity in Advanced Technology Use: Adaptive Structuration Theory. Organization Science 5(2), 121–147 (1994)
22. Orlikowski, W.J.: Using technology and constituting structures: A practice lens for studying technology in organizations. Resources, co-evolution and artifacts, pp. 255–305 (2008)
23. Orlikowski, W.J.: Sociomaterial practices: Exploring technology at work. Organization Studies 28(9), 1435–1448 (2007)
24. Leonardi, P.: When flexible routines meet flexible technologies: Affordance, constraint, and the imbrication of human and material agencies. MIS Quarterly 35(1), 147–167 (2011)
25. Germonprez, et.al.: Secondary design: A case of behavioral design science research. Journal of the Association for Information Systems (2011)
26. Winograd, T., Flores, F.: Understanding computers and cognition: A new foundation for design. Ablex Pub (1986)
27. Schön, D.A.: The reflective practitioner, vol. 1. Basic books (1999)
28. Rittel, H.W.: The reasoning of designers. IGP (1987)
29. Truex, D., Baskerville, R., Travis, J.: Amethodical systems development: the deferred meaning of systems development methods. Accounting, Management and Information Technologies 10(1), 53–79 (2000)

Evaluating Design Science Outputs – The Case of Enterprise Architecture Business Value Assessments

Martin Meyer and Markus Helfert

Dublin City University,
Glasnevin, Dublin 9, Ireland
{mmeyer,markus.helfert}@computing.dcu.ie

Abstract. In Design Science Research (DSR), evaluation of research outputs in form of design artifacts has been discussed in numerous publications. Many researchers have emphasized the criteria of utility for design artifacts. In this paper we use the case of Enterprise Architecture (EA) Management to demonstrate how design artefacts can be evaluated. Although EA has been extensively discussed in literature, the impact of the actual contribution of EA to the business value is not entirely understood. The focus of this paper is to evaluate our approach of EA business value assessment and demonstrate how we can effectively determine the relevant criteria and adapt an appropriate evaluation method.

Keywords: Design Science Research, Evaluation, Business Value Framework, Enterprise Architecture.

1 Introduction

The importance of evaluating research outputs has been emphasised and reiterated in many recent Design Science Research (DSR) discussions (Hevner et al. 2004; Iivari, 2007; Peffers et al. 2007; Hevner & Chatterjee 2010). Evaluation strategies and guidelines have been proposed, but yet evaluation of design artifacts is challenging. In our research we face the similar problem. We have developed an approach for assessing the business value of enterprise architecture management. In this paper we will discuss how this approach can be evaluated.

In today's corporate world, business strategies mostly revolve around business value, i.e. companies are business value driven. The assessment of business value spawned a myriad of approaches and is still a heavily discussed topic in literature and practice. Enterprise Architecture, a discipline with roots back to the 1980s, is a way to ensure a company's strategic business-IT alignment in order to leverage the desired level of business value by establishing an informed governance and strategic management function [1, 2]. Consequently, EA is crucial for an effective way to analyze and improve business, especially for large companies. Nevertheless, it is not a trivial task to assess EA in terms of business value.

In our work, we develop an Enterprise Architecture Business Value (EABV) assessment approach or EA benefits assessment approach respectively. More specifically,

M. Helfert et al. (Eds.): EDSS 2013, CCIS 447, pp. 135–145, 2014.

we build four IT artifacts that facilitate EABV assessments. In this paper, we focus on the DSR evaluation of our approach.

1.1   Motivation

The motivation for our research endeavor stems from the fact that the EA function in an organizational context is not entirely understood in terms of performance and business value [3-7]. Notably, we measure performance and communicate business value as proposed in [8]. A lot of the EA function performance falls into the category of intangible assets [9] and is therefore difficult to measure. Consequently, another purpose of this research is the development of appropriate metrics as this has not been done thoroughly enough in literature [3, 10]. But not only the finding of metrics alone is of our concern, we have to align them with appropriate goals according to the current strategy [11].When reviewing the literature on evaluation in a DSR context, we see that there is still a lot of room for suitable evaluation methods, especially when considering an organizational context.

But how do we actually evaluate such business value assessment approaches? To answer this question, we look at the relevant literature as well as business value assessment approaches. In addition, we design and evaluate our assessment approach within an organizational context and gain insights from subject matter experts in practice.

1.2   Research Methodology

For our work, we employ an adapted Design Science Research (DSR) methodology. We employ the DSR framework proposed in [12]. Our DSR artifact build cycle is based on [13, 14]. As can be seen in Fig. 1, we focus on the evaluation phase. For more on our adapted DSR methodology, refer to [15, 16].

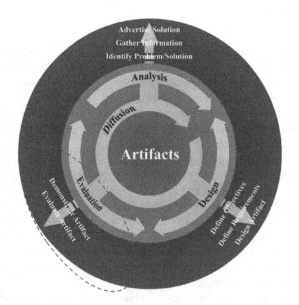

Fig. 1. DSR Artifact Build Cycle

Our research is conducted in collaboration with an industry partner which allows us to evaluate our IT artifacts in an organizational environment. For this paper, we gathered all relevant information and experience from practice as well as literature in order to find and execute the best possible EABV assessment evaluation in a DSR context. We had numerous expert interviews, workshops as well as surveys to propose an adapted assessment evaluation which we will outline more detailed in section 5.

2   Assessing Enterprise Architecture Business Value

The benefits associated with EA are manifold. We can find several approaches for assessing EA, e.g. the DeLone and McLean model is adapted in [17]. In [18] a Balanced Scorecard approach for EA measurement is employed. How certain EA practices and techniques influence EA benefits is discussed by [4]. The concept of maturity models is also applied to the domain of EA and there exist several frameworks and approaches for these kinds of assessments [19]. A general view on EA maturity is given in [20] and the link of EABV and EA maturity is described in [21]. Critical problems in EA are described in [3] although the sections about assessments and metrics are very limited. EA measurement drivers and enablers are discussed in [22] without going into detail about challenges and problems. EA management challenges in terms of agile solutions is examined in [23]. As business IT alignment (BITA) is a major EA driver, the assessment of it is discussed by various contributions [24-27].

2.1   EABV Assessment Types

EABV assessment is a continuous assessment because we employ a measurement process embedded into the daily EA operations, i.e. we constantly measure the EA operative performance. In contrast, a periodic assessment is an EA maturity assessment which captures the maturity of the overall EA capability. The EA capability determines how the EA function is executed and therefore has direct impact on the EA performance in operations. Nevertheless, statements about the business value of the EA function are tied to the operative performance since just attaching a maturity level to an EA capability tells us nothing about its actual impact in terms of EABV. We need to put the EA capability into practice. What we can do is to elaborate how EA performance is impacted by which EA capability.

Every EA assessment needs an input which is derived from the strategy. Strategy defines how the EA capability is set up and how it is executed. We need to derive goals for that purpose because we need to measure them whether successful or not. More on EA assessments including challenges and problems can be found in [11].

2.2   EABV Assessment Approach

Our EABV assessment approach consists of four IT artifacts; all designed using our Artifact Build Cycle. The main artifact is the EABV Framework. In order to provide a common understanding and a clear definition of what EABV is and how it is embedded into the organization, we built the EABV Model. Furthermore, we have the EABV Measurement Process which gathers relevant data about EABV and also provides means of reporting it in conjunction with the last artifact, an EABV Balanced Scorecard.

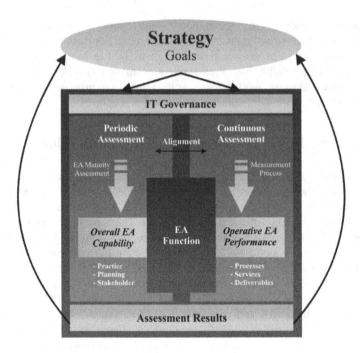

Fig. 2. EA Assessment Types

3   Design Science Evaluation

The evaluation of IT artifacts, which are in fact socio-technical entities within a certain environment, is of crucial importance [28, 29]. The purpose of this is to validate or confirm our artifacts respectively and hence our solution. It is necessary to justify the design and ensure that the intended approach satisfies the stakeholders. In its simplest form, evaluating a novel IT artifact means just it is working or producing adequate results [30].

In literature, we can find many different approaches for evaluations in a DSR context which are commonly bifurcating into ex ante and ex post evaluations. Thereby, ex ante evaluation happens before the decision to acquire or implement a new technology. A good example would be an investment decision. Such decisions are further classified in [31]. A whole evaluation framework is proposed in [32]. A classification of various evaluation methods based on a limited literature review is presented in [29]. By far the mostly employed method was the technical experiment to evaluate the technical performance rather than the real world performance. The reason for this lies in the specific selection of literature which delivers algorithms as most frequently built artifact type. The importance of utility and quality for artifact evaluation is highlighted in [33].

Nevertheless, what we did not find in the literature is an aggregated or combined evaluation, i.e. the evaluation of connected artifacts. These are not necessarily in a hierarchy as described in [34]. We therefore employ a method which also considers the actual organizational context in which we undertake our evaluation and the relationship between evaluated artifacts (cf. sec. 5).

3.1   Evaluation Perspectives

Each stakeholder or stakeholder group respectively possesses a different view on each IT artifact, i.e. he or she would have different preferences, opinions, and uses for a particular artifact [28]. Generally spoken, each stakeholder has different expectations of the benefits he or she will receive. Meeting stakeholder expectations poses a great challenge because goals and motivations are not always transparent and once known we must satisfy the stakeholder needs. For this purpose, we identified several stakeholder groups which are immediately affected by EA and are part of the EA assessment. These groups are based on previous periodic assessments conducted by our corporate partner. EA Managers are concerned about the strategy and high-level impact of EA. They are responsible for justifying the investments made and the overall quality of the EA outcome. EA Practitioners are Enterprise Architects at various levels of experience and are concerned about delivering quality output that is used by the EA Customers for their projects and programs. The stakeholder groups and their expected benefits are outlined in Table 1.

Table 1. Expected Stakeholder Benefits from EA

Stakeholder Group	Expected Benefits
EA Managers	• Positive ROI • Improved quality of EA function and corresponding output • Improved strategic decisions
EA Practitioners	• Reduced complexity in creating EA deliverables • Improved processes for service delivery
EA Customers	• Faster Time-to-Market for their services and products where EA services are consumed • Reduced complexity for their services and products

This list of perceived and reported benefits from EA is certainly not exhaustive but should demonstrate what stakeholders want to get out of the EA function and is based on the results of our survey as well as the literature review. A list with the most often perceived EA benefits can be found in [1], another list of EA benefits is composed in [4]. An example how different stakeholder groups perceive different EA benefits is illustrated in Fig. 3. As we can see, expected benefits overlap from for the chosen stakeholder groups. The perspectives determine the relevant goals stakeholders have regarding the EA function. As one of the main drivers for EA, the Business-IT Alignment (BITA) has been a major concern in recent literature [35, 36] and is a shared goal for all of our stakeholder groups. A more detailed take on stakeholder perception of EA is given in [37].

3.2   Evaluation Methods

Evaluation of design-based solutions has two major challenges. Firstly, a single individual cannot know all the criteria and constraints. Secondly, we must evaluate from different, sometimes conflicting, perspectives [38]. Before evaluating our approach, we need to choose the appropriate criteria to do so, e.g. functionality, completeness, consistency, accuracy, performance, reliability, usability, fit with organization, and

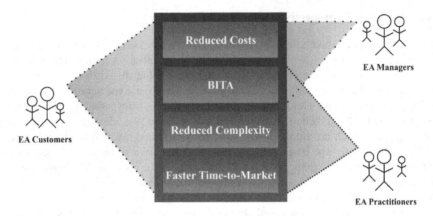

Fig. 3. Perspectives on EA benefits by stakeholder group

others more [12]. Generally, these criteria are derived from the artifact objectives [13]. We choose our criteria based on the artifact objectives and requirements. As should be already clear, the evaluation context of the IT artifacts is an organizational one. Different output has different criteria for different perspectives, e.g. we can view our artifacts as either products or processes [32]. This leads to different perception of our chosen stakeholder group and therefore different evaluation criteria apply. We will discuss a criterion-based evaluation in the next section.

4   Evaluation of the Enterprise Architecture Business Value Framework

In this section, we explain our chosen evaluation method and describe how we applied it to our EABV assessment approach.

4.1   Measurement and Analysis Infrastructure Diagnostic

The Measurement and Analysis Infrastructure Diagnostic (MAID) method [39] was designed to gain insights about how good a measurement and analysis system works in terms of certain criteria. In other words, an organization's data quality and means of information gathering and reporting can be assessed using this method. Consequently, it is the evaluation method of choice for our purposes. This method offers four phases, namely Collaborative Planning, Artifact Evaluation, On-Site Evaluation and Report Results. It has to be noted that the artifact in stage three is not an IT artifact in a DSR sense.

As a result, the method produces a detailed report about an organization's capability in measurement and analysis. This is the first of the two main MAID objectives with the other making recommendations for improvement. MAID is a collaborative effort and assigns clear roles and responsibilities for the evaluation team and other stakeholders from the assessed organization.

4.2   MAID Application for the EABV Assessment Approach

Having outlined the basic intent of MAID it is time to put it to action, i.e. we evaluate our EABV assessment approach. As we already mentioned in section 2, we have four different IT artifacts to assess EABV. We also outlined that there is little information about an aggregated evaluation in the DSR literature. When applying this method, we assess the whole approach based on chosen criteria and map them to the individual artifacts accordingly. MAID offers around 325 different criteria. Nevertheless, if an individual artifact needs to be evaluated even more detailed, we can choose additional criteria. The extent of such detailed evaluation has to be in accordance with the organization's time and budget constraints and hence the choice of adequate criteria is a crucial task. We now take a closer look at the four main phases of MAID.

Collaborative Planning
In this phase, we first need to establish the scope of our evaluation. We want to identify the relevant business needs and objectives as well as what exactly is to be evaluated. In our case, we want to evaluate our IT artifacts. Furthermore, we need to determine the participating stakeholders that contribute to the evaluation as well as their tasks. Another crucial part is the evaluation plan and schedule where we define inputs and outputs and tailor the MAID method to our needs and requirements. Hereby, we also look at budget and time constraints.

Artifact Evaluation
Artifacts in this phase are all relevant measurement and analysis documents, tools, and data repositories. Consequently, DSR artifacts are considered as MAID artifacts and serve as input for the method since we want to evaluate them.

We gather the relevant artifacts from the organizational context since our designed artifacts and their according output is already instantiated. We organize these artifacts and assign team members to evaluate them. The actual evaluation follows a criterion-based rating scale. The results are then reviewed for quality purposes. Finally, we need to prepare for the next phase, the On-Site Evaluation where we diffuse information material to support expert interviews and workshops following a detailed agenda.

On-Site Evaluation
This phase includes many meetings and interviews in order to examine relevant data repositories. Hereby, we kick off with an orientation meeting to ensure all stakeholders or MAID team member respectively are on the same page and share a common understanding on how the evaluation will be conducted. During further meetings, the chosen criteria are rated as an outcome of the evaluation.

Report Results
The final phase of our evaluation starts off with the analysis of the On-Site Evaluation results. From these, we derive key findings and report them accordingly. The reports are structured and organized according to stakeholder and organizational needs. Based

on these findings, we are able to plan the next steps. In other words, we determine where we want to go next within our artifact build cycle. For example, we could find out that our artifact design was not adequate to capture all the desired information which means that we need to step back to the Design phase (cf. Fig. 1) before we can conduct another evaluation.

Sample Criteria

The number of different criteria is enormous so we just give a sample mapping of how one of our artifacts is evaluated using a selection of relevant criteria. The artifact evaluated is the EABV Measurement process which defines what and how we will extract information for the EABV assessment. A phase of this process is the actual measurement planning. Hence, we focus on the measurement and analysis (M & A) planning category on organizational level [40]. The selected criteria are illustrated in Table 2. Other categories for criteria are e.g. project specific ones.

Table 2. Mapping of relevant criteria to the planning phase of the EABV Measurement Process

Category /Level/Number	Description
M & A Planning	
Organizational	
Level	
1.2	Organizational business goals are defined and documented.
1.3	Stakeholders of the business goals are explicitly defined.
1.4	Organizational business goals are expressed in measurable terms so progress toward achieving a goal can be assessed.
1.6	A measurement plan is documented.
1.8	The plan specifies the resources that are to be allocated for …
1.8.1	… staffing M & A personnel.
1.8.3	… data storage
1.8.4	… reporting (communicating)
1.9	Measurable business goals are documented in the plan.
1.10	A structured approach is followed to develop performance measures and measurement indicators.

5   Conclusion

In this paper, we presented an approach to evaluate an EABV assessment effort in a DSR context. The evaluation happens within the Evaluation phase of our Artifact Build Cycle. For this purpose, adapted a method to measure and analyze our four IT artifacts, namely the EABV Framework, the EABV Model, the EABV Measurement Process and the EABV Balanced Scorecard. Since we have not only one artifact, we are able to conduct an aggregated criterion-based evaluation with MAID. The level of detail for each of the artifacts is determined by the stakeholders and can be adapted according to organizational needs such as time and budget. We presented a mapping of sample criteria for one of the artifacts to illustrate the basis of our aggregated evaluation while still allowing for a detailed individual evaluation. Our evaluation effort is within an organizational context which allows us to incorporate valuable practitioner contribution along the insights gained from academic literature.

With this contribution, we managed to answer the question on how to evaluate an EABV assessment approach in an organizational and DSR context. We conducted a pilot assessment and researchers as well as practitioners found it to be reasonable and feasible.

Acknowledgments. This work is partly funded by the Irish Research Council (IRC).

References

1. Ross, J.W., Weill, P., Robertson, D.C.: Robertson, Enterprise Architecture as Strategy. Havard Business Press, Boston (2006)
2. Ahlemann, F., Legner, C., Schäfczuk, D.: Introduction. In: Ahlemann, F., et al. (eds.) Strategic Enterprise Architecture Management - Challenges, Best Practices, and Future Developments, pp. 1–34. Springer, Heidelberg (2012)
3. Kaisler, S.H., Armour, F., Valivullah, M.: Enterprise Architecting: Critical Problems. In: Proceedings of the 38th International Conference on System Sciences. IEEE, Hawaii (2005)
4. van Steenbergen, M., et al.: Achieving Enterprise Architecture Benefits: What Makes the Difference? In: 15th International Enterprise Distributed Object Computing Conference Workshops, Helsinki, Finland (2011)
5. Ross, J.W., Weill, P.: Understanding the Benefits of Enterprise Architecture. CISR Research Briefing (2005)
6. Shang, S., Seddon, P.B.: Assessing and Managing the Benefits of Enterprise Systems: The Business Manager's Perspective. Information Systems Journal, 271–299 (2002)
7. Fotini, M., Anthi-Maria, S., Euripidis, L.: ERP Systems Business Value: A Critical Review of Empirical Literature. In: Panhellenic Conference on Informatics. IEEE (2008)
8. Mitra, S., Sambamurthy, V., Westerman, G.: Measuring IT Performance and Communicating Value. In: MISQ Executive 2011, pp. 47–59 (2011)
9. Brynjolfsson, E., Hitt, L.M., Yang, S.: Intangible Assets: Computers and Organizational Capital. In: Brookings Papers on Economic Activity, pp. 137–181 (2002)
10. Vasconcelos, A., Sousa, P., Tribolet, J.: Information System Architecture Metrics: An Enterprise Engineering Evaluation Approach. Electronic Journal of Information Systems Evaluation, 91–122 (2007)
11. Meyer, M., Helfert, M.: Challenges and Problems of Enterprise Architecture Assessments - Lessons Learned. In: Proceedings of the 7th Mediterranean Conference on Information Systems 2012 (2012)
12. Hevner, A.R., March, S.T., Park, J.: Design Science in Information Systems Research. In: MIS Quaterly, pp. 75–105 (2004)
13. Österle, H., et al.: Memorandum on Design-oriented Information Systems Research. European Journal of Information Systems, 7–10 (2011)
14. Peffers, K., et al.: A Design Science Research Methodology for Information Systems Research. Journal of Management Information Systems, 45–77 (2008)
15. Meyer, M., Helfert, M., Donnellan, B., Kenneally, J.: Applying Design Science Research for Enterprise Architecture Business Value Assessments. In: Peffers, K., Rothenberger, M., Kuechler, B. (eds.) DESRIST 2012. LNCS, vol. 7286, pp. 108–121. Springer, Heidelberg (2012)

16. Meyer, M., Kenneally, J.: Applying design science research in enterprise architecture business value assessments. In: Helfert, M., Donnellan, B. (eds.) EDSS 2011. CCIS, vol. 286, pp. 151–157. Springer, Heidelberg (2012)

17. Niemi, E., Pekkola, S.: Adapting the Delone and McLean Model for the Enterprise Architecture Benefit Realization Process. In: Proceedings of the 42nd Hawaii International Conference on System Sciences. IEEE (2009)

18. Schelp, J., Stutz, M.: A Balanced Scorecard Approach to Measure the Value of Enterprise Architecture. Journal of Enterprise Architecture (2007)

19. Meyer, M., Helfert, M., O'Brien, C.: An Analysis of Enterprise Architecture Maturity Frameworks. In: Grabis, J., Kirikova, M. (eds.) BIR 2011. LNBIP, vol. 90, pp. 167–177. Springer, Heidelberg (2011)

20. Ross, J.W.: Creating a Strategic IT Architecture Competency: Learning in Stages. MISQ Executive 2(1), 31–43 (2003)

21. Bradley, R.V., et al.: The Role of Enterprise Architecture in the Quest for IT Value. MIS Quarterly Executive 10(2) (2011)

22. Murer, S., Bonati, B., Furrer, F.J.: Managed Evolution - A Strategy for Very Large Information Systems. Springer, Heidelberg (2011)

23. Buckl, S., et al.: Towards an Agile Design of the Enterprise Architecture Management Function. In: 15th IEEE International Enterprise Distributed Object Computing Conference Workshops, IEEE (2011)

24. Masak, D.: IT-Alignment: IT-Architektur und Organisation 2006. Springer (2006)

25. Luftman, J.N.: Assessing Business-IT Alignment Maturity. In: Communications of the Association for Information Systems 2000 (2000)

26. Zimmermann, S.: Governance im IT-Portfoliomanagement – Ein Ansatz zur Berücksichtigung von Strategic Alignment bei der Bewertung von IT. In: Wirtschaftsinformatik 2008, pp. 357–365 (2008)

27. van der Raadt, B., Hoorn, J.F., van Vliet, H.: Alignment and maturity are siblings in architecture assessment. In: Pastor, Ó., Falcão e Cunha, J. (eds.) CAiSE 2005. LNCS, vol. 3520, pp. 357–371. Springer, Heidelberg (2005)

28. Hevner, A., Chatterjee, S.: Design Research in Information Systems - Theory and Practice 2010. Springer (2010)

29. Peffers, K., Rothenberger, M., Tuunanen, T., Vaezi, R.: Design Science Research Evaluation. In: Peffers, K., Rothenberger, M., Kuechler, B. (eds.) DESRIST 2012. LNCS, vol. 7286, pp. 398–410. Springer, Heidelberg (2012)

30. Niederman, F., March, S.T.: Design Science and the Accumulation of Knowledge in the Information Systems Discipline. ACM Transactions on Management Information Systems (TMIS) 3(1) (2012)

31. Bannister, F., Remenyi, D.: Acts of Faith: Instinct, Value and IT Investment Decisions. Journal of Information Technology 15(3), 231–241 (2000)

32. Pries-Heje, J., Baskerville, R., Venable, J.: Strategies for Design Science Research Evaluation. In: ECIS (2008)

33. Helfert, M., Donnellan, B., Ostrowski, L.: The Case for Design Science Utility and Quality - Evaluation of Design Science Artifact within the Sustainable ICT Capability Maturity Framework. Systems, Signs & Actions 6(1), 46–66 (2012)

34. Simon, H.A.: The Sciences of the Artificial. MIT Press (1996)

35. Magoulas, T., et al.: Alignment in Enterprise Architecture: A Comparative Analysis of Four Architectural Approaches. Electronic Journal of Information System Evaluation 15(1), 53–62 (2012)

36. Schöenherr, M.: Towards a Common Terminology in the Discipline of Enterprise Architecture. In: Feuerlicht, G., Lamersdorf, W. (eds.) ICSOC 2008. LNCS, vol. 5472, pp. 400–413. Springer, Heidelberg (2009)
37. van der Raadt, B., Schouten, S., van Vliet, H.: Stakeholder Perception of Enterprise Architecture. In: Morrison, R., Balasubramaniam, D., Falkner, K. (eds.) ECSA 2008. LNCS, vol. 5292, pp. 19–34. Springer, Heidelberg (2008)
38. Bonnardel, N., Sumner, T.: Supporting Evaluation in Design. Acta Psychologica 91, 221–244 (1996)
39. Kasunic, M.: Measurement and Analysis Infrastructure Diagnostic 1.0: Method Definition Document. Software Engineering Institute (2010)
40. Kasunic, M.: Measurement and Analysis Infrastructure Diagnostic (MAID) Evaluation Criteria 1.0. Software Engineering Institute (2010)

Author Index